SHERLOCK
HOLMES'S
LONDON

SHERLOCK HOLMES'S LONDON

David Sinclair

ROBERT HALE · LONDON

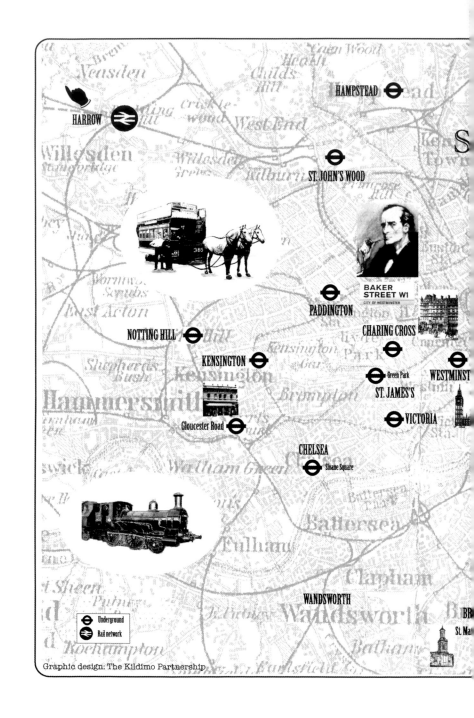

HARROW

HAMPSTEAD

ST. JOHN'S WOOD

BAKER
STREET W1
CITY OF WESTMINSTER

PADDINGTON

CHARING CROSS

NOTTING HILL

KENSINGTON

Kensington Park

Green Park

WESTMINST

ST. JAMES'S

Gloucester Road

VICTORIA

CHELSEA
Sloane Square

WANDSWORTH

BR
St. Ma

⊖ Underground
⊜ Rail network

Graphic design: The Kildimo Partnership

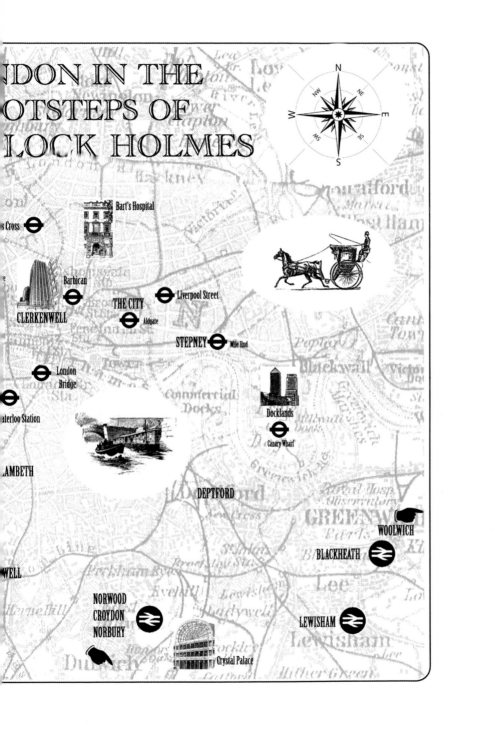

[LON]DON IN THE
[FO]OTSTEPS OF
[SHER]LOCK HOLMES

N
NW NE
W E
SW SE
S

Bart's Hospital

[s] Cross

CLERKENWELL
Barbican
THE CITY
Liverpool Street
Aldgate

STEPNEY Mile End

London Bridge

[W]aterloo Station

[L]AMBETH

Docklands
Canary Wharf

DEPTFORD
GREENW[ICH]
WOOLWICH
BLACKHEATH

[SE]LL

NORWOOD
CROYDON
NORBURY

LEWISHAM

Crystal Palace

A Sense of Place

HOW ARE WE to explain the continuing fascination with the exploits of Sherlock Holmes? What is it that motivates thousands of people each year to continue to buy the accounts of his cases as related in the reminiscences of Dr John H. Watson MD, late of the Army Medical Department, first published well over a century ago? Why is it that so many of those readers - or even people who have never read a Holmes story, but have merely heard of the most famous detective in the world – still search for the London rooms in Baker Street he shared with Dr Watson, or visit reconstructions of them at the Sherlock Holmes Museum or the Sherlock Holmes pub, or congregate round the statue of the supreme sleuth outside Baker Street Underground Station?

'The whole Sherlock Holmes saga is a triumphant illustration of art's supremacy over life,' observed the American writer Christopher Morley, founder of The Baker Street Irregulars and author of the standard introduction to *The Complete Sherlock Holmes*. 'Perhaps no fiction character ever created has become so real to his readers.'

Of course the main attraction arises from the innate characters of Holmes and Watson themselves. People admire Holmes's keen intelligence, his remarkable powers of observation and deduction, his tendency towards asceticism that is leavened by the human flaws of periodic depression and drug addiction. Watson is very he did in the 1890s. St Bartholomew's Hospital, where they first met, has expanded beyond anything they might have imagined, but its façade is as magnificent as ever. Even what must have been the very Bloomsbury house where, in 1896, Emilia Lucca hid herself away in a top-floor room is still standing, though modernized, and would serve as a reminder to a time-travelling Holmes and Watson of 'The Adventure of the Red Circle'.

Christopher Morley wrote:

> One of the blissful ways of passing an evening, when you encounter another dyed-in-the-blood addict, is to embark upon the happy discussion of minor details of Holmesiana. 'Whose gold watch was it that had been so mishandled?' one may ask; and the other counters with 'What was the book that Joseph Stangerson carried in his pocket?' Endless delicious minutiae to consider!

So it is with the places that form the backdrop to the endlessly readable cases, especially in London, where the bulk of them are set and of which Dr Watson's descriptions are so crucial to their enjoyment and timeless appeal. Nor are these merely subjects for discussion. The exciting thing about them is that we, as devotees of Sherlock Holmes, do not need to travel through time in order to follow the trail of our hero across contemporary London. We have read the cases many times but, if we do so again and apply the sort of analytical approach used by our hero himself, we shall be able to gaze with a high degree of certainty upon the scenes of many of the crimes and mysteries he solved in those far-off days.

Applying Holmes's and our own methods, and armed with a London A–Z, we should be able to identify where the body of young Cadogan West was placed on the roof of an Underground train in the case of the Bruce-Partington plans, or where the journalist Horace Harker found a corpse on his doorstep and set Holmes off on the investigation of the theft of six busts of the Emperor Napoleon.

We can find Holmes's first London lodgings in Montague Street and, not far away, the consulting rooms that must have been Dr

Watson's before he became an army medical officer. We can trace Holmes's footsteps down Endell Street to Covent Garden market on our way from the Alpha Tavern. We can see at least the buildings that used to be the hotels near Charing Cross where Sir Henry Baskerville and his malevolent shadow Stapleton stayed.

What we cannot actually see, we can imagine by fixing its former presence on what is in its place now. We can show once and for all precisely the location of the iconic 221B Baker Street, even though no trace of the building is left, and put an end to years of speculation and debate on the matter.

For these investigations, all our powers of deduction and reasoning will be required. Although Dr Watson's talents as a chronicler are almost on a par with those of Holmes as a detective, he is not always completely reliable. Sometimes he mixes up dates, so that we cannot be entirely sure which edition of the Post Office London Street Directory to consult in our search. This is important, given the sweeping changes that took place in the city between the 1880s and the turn of the century. Watson also has an inconsistent approach to his locations. Some, whether streets, buildings or mansion blocks, are to be found on the map. At other times Watson cloaks them in thin disguises that allow them easily to be identified by the amateur sleuth, though occasionally his camouflage is more difficult to penetrate.

The Langham Hotel, for instance, appears as itself in 'The Disappearance of Lady Frances Carfax'; the Mexborough Private Hotel in *The Hound of the Baskervilles* is disguise for what could have been at the time four or five such establishments in Craven Street, off the Strand; the Charing Cross Hotel, where the villain of 'The Adventure of the Bruce-Partington Plans' is arrested, is real enough. Similarly, Great George Street in Westminster and Campden Hill in Kensington are streets that can be walked along by anyone, but Caulfield Gardens, supposedly not far from Gloucester Road Underground station, is a pseudonym, though there are plenty of indications as to the identity and appearance of the real street it represents.

On some occasions, when Watson buries his scenes of crimes and the addresses of victims or perpetrators under layers of camouflage, his reasons for doing so are not always immediately apparent. I have found cases – as we shall see when we follow the trail of 'The Red-headed League' – in which a detailed description of a particular street appears to have been superimposed on another area quite some distance away, with Watson deliberately leading his readers on to the wrong track through his account of how the destination was reached. There are instances, too, of houses being mis-described to the extent that they cannot possibly have been exactly where Watson pretends they were. The writer's natural discretion obviously plays a part here, consideration for the sensitivities either of people involved in the investigation or else of subsequent residents of addresses that might attract unwelcome notoriety as a result of the doctor's revelations. Yet what was it that drove Watson in the same memoir to identify one real street and to dissemble mercilessly about others? Perhaps he was influenced by Holmes's habit of playing games with, or in some circumstances actually misleading, Inspector Lestrade and other Scotland Yard men by throwing out cryptic clues which, if correctly analysed, would lead to the truth. Like Holmes, Watson may be having fun by gambling on our interpretations of his leads being faulty.

Well, the doctor's mixture of genuine identity and various levels of disguise provides the most fascinating cases for the dedicated investigator, just as Holmes himself relished crimes that were above the commonplace – 'Give me problems, the most abstruse cryptogram, or the most intricate analysis,' as he cried in *The Sign of Four*.

Where and what was the real model for the Diogenes Club, second home of Holmes's brother Mycroft? What was the Saxe-Coburg Square of 'The Red-headed League' really called? If we strip away Watson's disguise, how can we identify the square in Brixton where the unfortunate Lady Frances Carfax was held prisoner? Is the villa in St John's Wood where Irene Adler lived still there? Can we follow 'The Man with the Twisted Lip' to the site of his opium den near London Bridge? As for Dr Watson, he tells us that at one point he lived and practised medicine in Kensington, but are there any indications that will lead us to where his house might have been?

Finding these places, and taking readers to them when possible, is the purpose of this book. Analysing the information provided by Dr Watson, whether clear or in code, and armed with the invaluable Post Office Directories and contemporary maps, the book will identify the scenes of crimes, the homes of villains and victims, the restaurants and concert halls where Holmes and Watson took their ease and all the other locations that feature in the London stories. It will recall the sights and sounds of the days of Holmes and Watson and compare them with what is to be found in those places today, sometimes still the actual buildings described in the stories. It will make journeys by hansom cab, brougham and four-wheeler – or on foot in many cases – and explain how to reach the destinations in twenty-first-century London by taxi, bus or Tube.

Holmes and Watson may be long dead, but the thrill of the chases they knew can, with close reading and much imagination, be recreated. The trails will take us, case by case, from the mansions of Mayfair, through the terraces of Kensington and the bustle of the West End to the market in Covent Garden and the hotels and theatres of the Strand, out to the City and beyond to the East End. We shall travel south of the river to Brixton, Lewisham, Norwood and Streatham, and north to St John's Wood, Hampstead and beyond. The game is still afoot.

We begin with the most comprehensive tour of London in any of the Sherlock Holmes cases, the veritable odyssey by road and the high-speed chase eastward down the Thames that make *The Sign of Four* so gripping.

of the fact that, as one of the highest districts in Greater London, it has remained inaccessible directly by train. To Watson this really was the countryside. 'We had left the damp fog of the great city behind us,' he observed and it was so dark when they arrived at nearly eleven o'clock that Sholto had to take down one of the side-lamps from the carriage to guide their way to the house.

> Pondicherry Lodge stood in its own grounds and was girt round with a very high stone wall topped with broken glass. A single iron-clamped door formed the only means of entrance ... Inside, a gravel path wound through desolate grounds to a huge clump of a house, square and prosaic, all plunged in shadow save where a moonbeam struck one corner and glimmered in a garret window. The vast size of the building, with its gloom and its deathly silence, struck a chill to the heart.

As it turned out, they were too late to hear the story of Bartholomew Sholto, whose lifeless form they found in his bedroom, or to inspect the Agra treasure, which had evidently been stolen. Holmes's careful examination revealed that the man had been killed by a poisoned dart, that one of the killers had been a man with a wooden leg and that his accomplice must have been a pygmy. He also noticed that the one-legged man had stepped in creosote, which provided the opportunity of finding him – 'I know a dog that would follow that scent to the world's end.' And so the chase across London resumed.

Watson was dispatched in a cab to take Miss Morstan home to what he called vaguely 'Lower Camberwell' and then to fetch for Holmes the mongrel with the sensitive nose that was to be provided by a man named Sherman 'down near the water's edge at Lambeth'. The address is given as 3 Pinchin Lane, one of 'a row of shabby, two-storied brick houses in the lower quarter of Lambeth'. Quite what the doctor means by that location is unclear, but we might assume that it lay between Lambeth Bridge and Westminster Bridge, probably on the eastern side of Albert Embankment, which was, of course, not the collection of large buildings we see there today. There was no Pinchin Lane in the district, or anywhere else in Lambeth for that matter, so Watson had obviously decided to apply one of his disguises. He might have been talking about Ferry Street, almost at the end of Lambeth Bridge, where there was a row of small houses in a cul-de-sac that has long since been demolished.

Wherever he actually found it, the doctor returned to Pondicherry Lodge with Toby the dog at three o'clock in the morning. The dog was given the scent of the creosote and there began one of the most remarkable parts of the tour of London – 'a six-mile trudge', as Holmes described it, with what turned out to be some understatement.

Led by the dog, Holmes and Watson set off through the 'half-rural villa-lined roads' of Norwood towards Streatham then struck north through Brixton and Camberwell until they found themselves at Kennington Oval. Originally established in 1845 on land owned by the Duchy of Cornwall (which it still is), the Oval had already become a celebrated international cricket ground by the 1880s, the first ever Test Match in England having been played there between England and Australia. Indeed this was where The Ashes were invented, when *The Sporting Times* announced the death of English cricket after a crushing defeat by the Australians in 1882 and suggested that 'the body will be cremated and the ashes taken to Australia'.

Coming from the direction Watson described, Toby the dog must have led them to this spot via Magee Street from the northern end of Brixton Road. Then Watson says that they were 'borne away through the side streets to the east' of the Oval, which would have taken them past the gasworks and into Montford Place, because they emerged in Kennington Lane. Even now it is possible to follow their progress on foot, despite extensive rebuilding in the area, and a few of the houses they would have passed in Montford Place are still there.

Turning towards the river on Kennington Lane, the two men and the dog followed their quarry left into Bond Street (now Bondway) and thence, near the railway bridge that still carries trains into Vauxhall and Waterloo Stations, into Miles Street. That brought them out on to Wandsworth Road, where their four-wheeler had taken them on the second stage of their journey the previous evening. After some hesitation here, Toby picked up the scent once more and led them towards the river and Nine Elms Lane where, as Watson reports, 'we came to Broderick and Nelson's large timber yard just past the White Eagle tavern' and the trail reached its end. He is indulging in fiction again. In fact the tavern was called the White Swan and the timber mill was owned by Lloyd & Company, both of them roughly on what is now the site of a block of luxurious apartments backing on to the Thames.

This was a false scent, however, leading to nothing more revealing than an empty creosote barrel in the timber yard. As Holmes explained: 'If you consider how much creosote is carted about London in one day, it is no great wonder that our trail should have been crossed. It is much used now, especially for the seasoning of wood. Poor Toby is not to blame.'

They made their way back to what the doctor calls Knight's Place, which I have been unable to identify. It does not appear in the Post Office London Street Directory for the period and there seems to be no trace of it on contemporary maps, but Watson suggests it was off Wandsworth Road. This must mean it was at the Vauxhall end of Nine Elms Lane, because the mass of railway lines leading to the Nine Elms Goods Depot would have prevented their reaching Wandsworth Road from anywhere else. Whatever Knight's Place was really called – perhaps Watson's memory was playing tricks and he was thinking of Knight's Walk in Kennington – it has disappeared now under the vast site of the flower market that moved from Covent Garden to Nine Elms in 1974. At all events, this misnaming seems to have put Watson off his own scent because the mixture of real and fictional streets continues with the rest of their search.

He reports that Toby led them towards the riverside through Belmont Place and into Princes Road, then Broad Street. The last two are genuine names, but there is no sign of Belmont Place. What they must actually have done is retrace their steps to Vauxhall Cross, pass under the railway bridge and turn left into Auckland Street, which would lead them through a series of other streets to Princes Road. Today, this is called Black Prince Road

The old Doulton pottery factory, which still stands at the corner of Lambeth High Street, close to the Thames. Holmes and Watson passed it on their way down Broad Street (now Prince Road) as they followed Jonathan Small towards the river in *The Sign of Four*

(there was and still is a public house there called the Black Prince). The road runs from Kennington Road down to Albert Embankment and the headquarters of the Fire Brigade, but in 1888 the lower part of it was known as Broad Street, so in this case Watson was being entirely accurate.

Holmes and Watson would have been too engrossed in their task to notice it, but in Broad Street, at the corner of Lambeth High Street, they would have passed the famous pottery and sanitary ware factory of Doulton & Co., later Royal Doulton. The High Street is now a mere shadow of its nineteenth-century self, but part of the wonderful Doulton building is still there, with its striking frieze above the door. The factory had begun by making stoneware drainpipes and other sanitary materials, but by 1846 it was

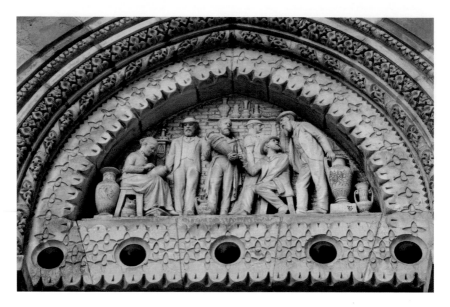

George Tinworth's fine terra-cotta frieze above the entrance
of the Doulton factory

producing art pottery designed mainly by former students of the
Lambeth School of Art. It became famous for Doultonware, which
is stoneware with a salt glaze used among other things for the
facings of buildings, and also for Lambeth Faience, a process of
double-firing that was ideal for the addition of painted decoration.
The factory's terracotta work was also highly prized and it is a fine
example of this by George Tinworth that graces the closed
entrance of what remains of the factory.

Having reached the riverside at the bottom of Broad Street,
Toby dashed across the Embankment and headed towards
Lambeth Bridge until he reached a small wooden wharf. 'We are
out of luck,' said Holmes. 'They have taken a boat here.' Walk
along Albert Embankment today, between Lambeth and Vauxhall
Bridges, and you will find near the junction with Black Prince
Road the sophisticated successor to what must have been the
'rude landing stage' from which the killers of Bartholomew Sholto
made their escape downriver.

A dock is marked at this spot on contemporary maps, but no
boatyard is listed, although there must have been one. Watson no

doubt changed the name of the owner of 'a small brick house, with a wooden placard slung out of the second window' that read 'Mordecai Smith – Boats to hire by the hour or day'. The boatman was not at home, but when Holmes questioned his wife she revealed that Smith had sailed off in his steam launch *Aurora* with a one-legged man as his passenger. Holmes and Watson had no alternative but to return to Baker Street to organize a search for the *Aurora* among 'the perfect labyrinth of landing-places' along the river.

They took a wherry across the Thames, landing, according to Watson, near the old Millbank Prison, which had already been closed but was still very much a London landmark. In the *Hand-Book of London* by the Scottish writer Peter Cunningham, published in 1850, the prison was described as:

A mass of brickwork equal to a fortress, on the left bank of the Thames, close to Vauxhall Bridge; erected on ground bought in 1799 of the Marquis of Salisbury, and established pursuant to 52 Geo. III., c.44, passed Aug 20th, 1812. It was designed by Jeremy Bentham, to whom the fee-simple of the ground was conveyed, and is said to have cost the enormous sum of half a million sterling. The external walls form an irregular octagon, and enclose upwards of sixteen acres of land. Its ground-plan resembles a wheel, the governor's house occupying a circle in the centre, from which radiate six piles of building, terminating externally in towers. The ground on which it stands is raised but little above the river, and was at one time considered unhealthy. It was first named 'The Penitentiary', or 'Penitentiary House for London and Middlesex', and was called 'The Millbank Prison' pursuant to 6 & 7 of Victoria, c.26. It is the largest prison in London. Every male and female convict sentenced to transportation in Great Britain is sent to Millbank previous to the sentence being executed. Here they remain about three months under the close inspection of the three inspectors of the prison, at the end of which time the inspectors report to the Home Secretary, and recommend the place of transportation. The number of persons in Great Britain and Ireland condemned to transportation every year amounts to about 4000. So far as the accommodation of the prison permits, the separate system is adopted.

To which Dickens's *Dictionary of London*, appearing nearly thirty years later, added: 'The building is intended to hold 1,000 prisoners, and cost half-a-million, which, with ground rent, &c., represents an outlay per head for rent, &c, of about £50 per annum, or, as the prison is rarely more than half full, practically not far short of £100.'

No doubt the decline of the transportation of criminals as a punishment, which had ended by 1870, and the costs of maintaining prisoners in this vast building, when other places had been provided in London where they could be incarcerated, contributed to the closure of Millbank in 1886. It was demolished a couple of years after Watson remarked on it and in its place was built the National Gallery of British Art, which was later renamed the Tate Gallery after the sugar millionaire Henry Tate, its chief benefactor, and is now known as Tate Britain. A fragment of one buttress of the grim old prison has been preserved on Millbank, near the steps down to the river where until 1867 prisoners had boarded ships for transportation to Australia. A plaque on the relic reads: 'Near this site stood Millbank Prison which was opened in 1816 and closed in 1890. This buttress stood at the head of the river steps from which, until 1867, prisoners sentenced to transportation embarked on their journey to Australia.' It must have been at the jetty where this had happened that Holmes and Watson disembarked after crossing the river.

At this point, though, Watson's geography becomes somewhat suspect again. He has Holmes calling at the post office in Great Peter Street, Westminster, to send a wire summoning the gang of street urchins that became known as the Baker Street Irregulars whom he wanted to recruit in the search for the missing steam launch. At that time, however, and for many years afterwards, there was no post office in Great Peter Street, or Great Smith Street or yet Great College Street, all of which are very close to each other, so it cannot have been merely a mistake in the name on Watson's part.

The nearest post offices I could find in the area in 1888 were at the corner of Tothill Street and Victoria Street, across the road from the Sanctuary at Westminster Abbey, and in Horseferry

Road, which runs from the northern end of Lambeth Bridge towards Victoria. The latter was probably the one Watson was referring to because it was closest to where they had disembarked from the wherry. What probably happened was that, having sent the telegram, they walked from Regent Place at the end of Horseferry Road to Victoria Street in order to be sure of being able to find a cab at that hour of the morning. They would have passed the end of Great Peter Street on their way and we might assume that Watson's memory must have played a trick on him when he came to write down the details of the case.

So we are in the West End once more, having been eastward to the Strand and back again and then completed a pretty comprehensive tour of south-western suburbs. Our journey in the footsteps of Sherlock Holmes on the case of *The Sign of Four* is very far from over, however.

To be sure, there was something of an interlude as Holmes's urchins scoured the riverbanks for the *Aurora* while the detective himself researched the poison used in the dart that had killed Sholto and the possible identity of the one-legged man's small accomplice. He had already identified the man they had attempted to follow as Jonathan Small. He had served in the army in India with the fathers of the Sholtos and Miss Morstan and had been involved in the theft of the Agra treasure, which had subsequently been stolen from him by old Sholto. As a result of his new inquiries, Holmes concluded that Small's companion, and the actual killer, was an Andaman Islander, one of a race 'naturally hideous, having large, misshapen heads, small fierce eyes, and distorted features'.

At the same time, Watson was not entirely idle. Romantically attracted to Miss Morstan – she would later become his wife – he went over to Camberwell to spend the day with her, returning Toby the dog to his owner in Lambeth on the way. The following day, Holmes also became active again, disguising himself as an old seaman and visiting sixteen boatyards along the Thames until he found one into which, as he had suspected, the *Aurora* had been brought for minor repairs. He learned that the vessel was to be collected that evening … and the chase for the Agra treasure was

A new police launch, the forerunner of this modern version, must have been used by Holmes, Watson and Inspector Jones when they raced along the Thames in pursuit of Jonathan Small and the Agra treasure in *The Sign of Four*

on again. This time he needed the help of the police so, after a pleasant dinner at the Baker Street apartment, he, Watson and Inspector Athelney Jones of Scotland Yard set off for Westminster Pier, where a fast police launch would be waiting for them.

In those days the Thames Division of the Metropolitan Police patrolled the river mainly in rowing boats, but the service had recently been equipped with two steam launches and one of them had evidently been placed at Inspector Jones's disposal. Perhaps it was even the *Alert*, which featured in an article about the river police published in *The Strand Magazine* in 1891. An engraving of the launch can be seen in the museum at the headquarters of what is now called the Marine Support Unit at Wapping. The pier at which the launch waited, close to Westminster Bridge, is still important today, though mainly as a boarding point for the pleasure cruisers that carry so many tourists up and down the Thames, and by means of which the dedicated Sherlock Holmes aficionado can follow at least part of the famous river pursuit of Jonathan Small and the Andaman Islander.

It was almost sunset when the police launch cast off from Westminster Pier and the last section of Dr Watson's guide to London began. What they would have seen in the gathering twilight, on both sides of the river, was almost unimaginably different from the views offered to the passenger on the modern cruiser.

The left bank between Westminster Bridge and Blackfriars Bridge is probably the section of the riverside least changed in appearance, apart from the traffic clogging Victoria Embankment. There is an elegant new footbridge at Charing Cross, but the gardens near Embankment Underground station are much as they were in Holmes's day, as are Somerset House and The Temple, even if many of the buildings surrounding them have altered radically. On the right bank, however, it is a completely different story. For one thing, the huge London Eye, the giant observation wheel in the Jubilee Gardens near Waterloo Station, would have astonished Watson in 1888, since it was five years before even the prototype of such a structure would be built in America and a further decade until the giant Riesenrad Ferris wheel appeared in the Prater park in Vienna. What Watson would have seen as they passed the spot was a series of commercial wharves – Maudley's, Lucas's, Holland's – and the Government Military Stores for India.

As the boat passed under Charing Cross Bridge, the smells of hops and malt from the Lion Brewery would have been wafting towards them, then the tall shot-tower of Walker and Company's leadworks would have come into view, where the Queen Elizabeth Hall now stands. There was another leadworks after Waterloo Bridge and a further series of busy wharves running all the way to Blackfriars, where today we have the Royal Festival Hall and the London Television Centre.

After Blackfriars Bridge, the cityscape on both sides of the river would cause Watson's jaw to drop if he could see it today: Tate Modern, the Millennium Bridge and the towering concrete, glass and steel office blocks of the City. He would wonder what had happened to Queenhithe Dock and what the great buildings are where Bell Wharf and all the other ship-handling facilities were located in his time. At least he would be reassured by the sight of the cupola of St Paul's, where, he noted from the police launch, 'the last rays of the sun were gilding the cross upon the summit'.

What would strike him most on a twenty-first-century voyage along this part of the Thames would be the quietness of it all. Although traffic has returned to the Thames in recent years, it consists mainly of pleasure boats, tourist cruisers, numbers of barges (transporting rubbish, among other things) and some river buses. In the age of Holmes and Watson, the river would have been crowded with ships' masts, lightermen plying their trade, wharfingers and dockers, noise and smoke and activity. From London Bridge eastward Watson would today recognize Billingsgate Market, the shell of which at least remains, and the bulk of the Custom House, not to mention the outlines of the warehouses on the south bank, even if they are now used as offices, shopping centres and restaurants and the docks that served them have disappeared. Then the familiar shapes of the Tower of London and Tower Bridge would come into view.

It was close to the Tower, on what the doctor calls the Surrey side of the river, that Holmes had found the boatyard where Mordecai Smith's *Aurora* had been under repair.

> *'And there is the Aurora, and going like the devil,' cried Holmes. 'Full speed ahead, engineer.'*

With a high-speed pursuit now under way, Watson would not have had much time to admire the views from the river. They dashed into the Pool of London between Wapping and Bermondsey, passing the headquarters of the Thames Division on their port side. Then they were into Limehouse Reach and the long sweep of the river that rounds the Isle of Dogs. Watson did note the presence of the West India Docks – what would he have made of Canary Wharf and South Quay, the Docklands Light Railway and all the other space-age developments that have transformed what had been the first commercial wet docks in London and at one stage had been capable of berthing six hundred ships?

The *Aurora*, heading for Gravesend and a waiting ship, led them rapidly on the curving course of the river into Greenwich Reach and on to Blackwall, round the peninsula where the controversial Millennium Dome was to be built a little more than a century later. Meanwhile, just four years after the events Watson was describing, work would begin on the construction of what would be for a time the world's longest underwater tunnel at Blackwall, which is, of course, still an important river crossing.

'At Greenwich we were about three hundred paces behind them,' Watson recalled. 'At Blackwall we could not have been more than two hundred and fifty. I have coursed many creatures in many countries during my checkered career, but never did sport give me such a wild thrill as this mad, flying man-hunt down the Thames.'

On they sped, passing the Royal Victoria Dock, the first to be built in London specifically to accommodate the large steamships that were becoming the staple of international trade, and the then new Royal Albert Dock, considered at the time to be among the finest in the world. Holmes was already familiar with the place, having traced to it the barque *Lone Star*, whose captain and two mates brought havoc to the Openshaw family in the case of 'The Five Orange Pips'. Holmes was too late. The ship had already sailed, but only to meet its doom in the wild Atlantic and leaving the investigation as one of those which Watson said had never been entirely cleared up and probably never would be.

Now, of course, the Royal Albert Dock sits alongside the London City Airport and is used mainly for watersports. Between it and the Royal Victoria Dock today we find the Thames Barrier, built to protect London from flooding, which would have staggered Holmes and Watson. Even what we now think of as the venerable Woolwich Ferry was a project for the future as the two launches raced into Woolwich Reach: the free service did not start until 1889.

By this time they were a very long way east, with Barking Levels and Barking Creek on the north side and on the opposite bank the dreary and dangerous marshes where work would begin on the building of the new town of Thamesmead in the 1960s. It was here, where great stretches of the Barking marshes do not look so very different now from the way they would have appeared to Watson in the searchlight of their police boat, that the chase ended with the

CHAPTER TWO

Bloomsbury to Baker Street

I T WAS IN the autumn of 1876, so far as we can tell, that the young Sherlock Holmes came down from university and settled in London to pursue the scientific researches that were to become such a crucial element of his unparalleled success as a private detective. Forensic science was in its infancy, but the clear-thinking Holmes had seen from his studies of criminology how important it was going to be and he realized that mastery of the subject would set him apart from the legion of other 'private agents' who operated in London at the time, mainly from Craig Court in Whitehall.

Fresh from academe and having grown up in the country, the 22-year-old Holmes was able to set up home in a part of London that contained both elements of study and a certain rustic quality – Bloomsbury. As he told Dr Watson in 'The Musgrave Ritual', when describing his early days in London: 'I had rooms in Montague Street, round the corner from the British Museum, and there I waited, filling in my too abundant leisure time by studying all those branches of science which might make me more efficient.'

Not only was the famous Reading Room of the British Museum a few minutes' walk away, but the University of London, with its medical school and laboratories, also lay within a few streets. Perhaps most importantly, the headquarters of the Pharmaceutical Society of Great Britain were at the time just round the corner in Great Russell Street. It was in this building that Holmes must have spent a good deal of his time, becoming, as Dr Watson recorded, a leading expert in 'belladonna, opium and poisons generally'. Perhaps it was there, too, that Holmes became familiar with the effects of cocaine and worked out that a 'seven per cent solution' could relieve his black moods without causing him permanent damage.

The Pharmaceutical Society had been in existence for more than thirty years, and had been granted its royal charter, when Holmes arrived there to study. As its title suggests, it was founded essentially to train pharmacists but an important part of its course consisted of the study of the chemical properties of plants and the pharmacological aspects of medicine. These were certainly what would have most interested Sherlock Holmes. Among the founders of the institution was William Allen, a noted scientist and Fellow of the Royal Society, whose own pharmaceutical company grew to become one of Britain's largest firms in the industry, Allen and Hanburys. Though the Pharmaceutical Society held its royal charter from 1843, it was not until 1988 that the word 'Royal' was added to its name by permission of the Queen. At the time of writing, the Royal Pharmaceutical Society, the head-quarters of which are now in Lambeth, remains the regulatory body for all British pharmacists but there are plans to form a new professional organization that might see the role of the Society diminished in this respect.

The presence of the Pharmaceutical Society, however, was only part of the attraction of Bloomsbury for Sherlock Holmes. Montague Street is a pleasant, sunlit terrace of late Georgian houses that runs between the attractive green spaces of Russell Square and Bloomsbury Square, each with the lawns, trees and wildlife that would have offered the young man relief from the bustle, noise and dirt of mid-Victorian London. Even today, Russell Square, though in the middle of a busy one-way traffic system, is something of a haven and much loved by local residents, commuting workers, university students and the tourists who throng the many hotels in the district. Bloomsbury Square, lying between Great Russell Street and the now crowded, often blocked traffic artery of Bloomsbury Way, has lost much of its former charm

Montague Street, Bloomsbury, is where Holmes had his lodgings when he first arrived in London. The building that had been leased by one of his female relatives is entered by the green door on the right of the entrance to the hotel of which it is now part

and virtually all its glory, having been excavated to provide a large underground carpark. Yet it is still somehow uplifting to turn the corner where the Royal Pharmaceutical Society's old building stands and find an open, tree-dotted square.

What evidence we have strongly suggests that it was at number 24 Montague Street where Holmes lodged. The four-storey house is now part of the small and discreet Ruskin Hotel, but in 1875 it was leased by the Bedford Estate to a certain Mrs Holmes for seven years. The lady must surely have been the grandmother or the aunt or some other relation of Sherlock Holmes and, though it is doubtful that she took the house with her then undergraduate relative specifically in mind, it would surely have been proposed as the obvious place to accommodate him as he sought to make his way in the world. One might even assume that, as a member of the family, he did not pay rent for his rooms in Montague Street since, by his own admission, he could not afford by himself the three guineas or so that was being asked for the apartment he had seen in Baker Street, which was what would prompt him to go into partnership with Dr Watson in the first place.

He would not have been earning a great deal of money, if any, during those early days. His investigative powers were called upon by only a handful of clients, mostly friends and acquaintances from his university days from whom he would have been reluctant to demand professional fees. Indeed, his very first case after his arrival in London, 'The Gloria Scott', resulted in his friend Victor Trevor fleeing to the colonies with a broken heart after the sudden death of his father.

Holmes must have taken some cases for which he was paid, however. There is some evidence, as we shall see later, that even as a young man he had contact with the developing police detective force, and it seems that he might have been somehow involved in the pursuit of the notorious cat burglar Charlie Peace, who was responsible for a wave of housebreaking in South London in 1877 and 1878. In the main, though, these years were devoted to perfecting his techniques as an investigator and acquiring the forensic knowledge that would later serve him so well.

Meanwhile, as Holmes was striving to establish himself in his chosen profession of 'consulting detective', the other and somewhat older half of the legendary partnership was completing his own studies and apparently practising medicine in Bloomsbury, just a few hundred yards from Montague Street. Dr John H. Watson obtained his MD at the University of London medical school – on the other side of the British Museum in Gower Street – in 1878. That, however, would have been his final qualification, necessary for him to achieve his ambition of being accepted into the army with the status of an officer and a gentleman. Before he had received that qualification, there would have been nothing to prevent him from treating patients and securing an income so as to allow him to complete his studies and reach the standard required by the army.

It is on record that in 1877 a Dr John Watson had consulting rooms at number 6 Southampton Street, now known as Southampton Place, which runs from the south side of Bloomsbury

This building in what was Southampton Street and is now called Southampton Place, off Bloomsbury Square, is where we know a Dr Watson practised in 1877, some three years before Holmes and Watson met at St Bartholomew's Hospital

Square down to High Holborn. This surely cannot be a mere coincidence. It must be the case that Holmes and Watson found themselves unknowingly living alongside each other in Bloomsbury long before their Baker Street days.

There is every chance that Watson would have walked past Holmes's front door on his way to Gower Street, or that the two men might even have seen each other as they took their ease in one of the many inns and restaurants in the Holborn area. Watson reveals that the Holborn Restaurant was one of his favourite eating places and it seems inconceivable that Holmes, who was fond of good food, as will become obvious, would not have sampled the fare offered in the impressive dining-rooms of the famous restaurant frequented by the Prince of Wales and his wealthy and aristocratic companions. The restaurant is long gone, its corner site now occupied by a Sainsbury's supermarket, but the style of the

BLOOMSBURY TO BAKER STREET

NatWest Bank building next door in High Holborn gives an idea of what it must have looked like.

What does remain, a few yards away, is the marvellous Princess Louise pub, built just five years before Holmes's arrival in the district. Refurbished in 1891, the place was remarkable for its extravagant tiled interiors, ornate plasterwork and yards of gilt mirrors, and it would have been very odd if Holmes and Watson had not stood at its elegant bar or partaken of its generous luncheons. Once threatened with demolition, this wonderful piece of Victorian decoration is now Grade II Listed and has been fully restored to its former magnificence.

At all events, whether or not the paths of Holmes and Watson ever crossed during this period, it was to be some years before they actually came to know each other. Towards the end of 1878, Watson left for training as an army surgeon at Netley Hospital in Hampshire, presumably travelling there daily by train from Waterloo Station. It has been established that the practice of Dr Watson in Southampton Street was retained for some time and it would have been easy enough for him to reach the station in a short journey down Little Queen Street (now Kingsway) and over Waterloo Bridge. His training course successfully completed, Watson left for India in 1879, having been assigned to the Fifth Northumberland Fusiliers.

His military career was destined to be short, however. Transferred to the Royal Berkshire Regiment, he was seriously wounded at the disastrous battle of Maiwand, during the Second Afghan War, in July 1880, and evacuated to Peshawar. There he contracted enteric fever: 'For months my life was despaired of, and when at last I came to myself and became convalescent, I was so weak and emaciated that a medical board determined that not a day should be lost in sending me back to England.'

Watson arrived in London in November 1880, but he did not return to Bloomsbury. Unfit to work after his illness, he either gave up or reassigned his lease on 6 Southampton Street, perhaps to another medical man or else to one of the many solicitors who had their offices in the street – that is, if he had not already done so when he went to India. With no home to go to and, as he says himself, 'neither kith nor kin in England', he took up temporary residence at a private hotel in the Strand, sustained by an army pension of eleven shillings and sixpence a day, or a fraction more than £4 a week. (Before decimalization, £1 was divided into twenty shillings, each containing twelve pence. One old shilling is therefore the equivalent of five new pence. A guinea is £1 and 1s/5p.)

The hotel he describes as 'pretentious and expensive', so was he staying at the Charing Cross Hotel by the railway station? Opened in 1865 and extended a couple of years before Watson's return to London, it remained the best hotel in the Strand until the opening of the Savoy in 1889. If that was indeed where the doctor took up residence, it would have cost him rather more than half his pension, plus meals, and might explain why 'so alarming did the state of my finances become that I soon realized that I must either leave the metropolis and rusticate somewhere in the country, or that I must make a complete alteration in my style of living'. Yet there were plenty of other hotels in the Strand – the Wellington, near the Lyceum Theatre, or Haxell's Royal Exeter, the Queen's Head Hotel or the Windsor. The now unemployed doctor might have boarded weekly at one of them for as little as thirty-five shillings, but such an establishment would never have been thought of as pretentious and, as we shall see, Watson seems to have had rather expensive tastes.

The Wellington would certainly have been just a short walk from his favourite Holborn Restaurant. On the other hand, the Windsor Hotel (which had its own restaurant, which might have earned it something of a reputation for pretension), just west of Bedford Street, was within easy reach of another of the doctor's favourite watering-holes, the Criterion Bar at Piccadilly Circus, where the fateful meeting took place that was to lead him to Sherlock Holmes.

Whichever hotel it was, Watson could not afford to stay there indefinitely. As luck would have it, Holmes, too, was obliged at that time to consider a change in his style of living. The lease taken by his female relative on number 24 Montague Street had a little more than a year to run, and it may be that she was already making plans to move somewhere else, possibly even to leave

London. On the other hand, Holmes's habits were such that there might well have been a certain amount of tension in the household. As he told Watson in the course of their first meeting, he smoked strong tobacco, 'I get in the dumps at times, and don't open my mouth for days on end', he played the violin and 'I generally have chemicals about, and occasionally do experiments'. Any one of those activities would have been likely to strain the nerves of a genteel Victorian matron, but taken together one can easily imagine that they would have become unbearable to her.

Like Watson, Holmes was not exactly flush with cash and it had become obvious to him that he was going to have to find someone with whom he could share any new 'diggings'. The flat he had seen in Baker Street was perfectly suited to sharing, situated on the first floor and with 'two comfortable bedrooms and a large airy sitting room', while the price asked by the landlady, Mrs Hudson, included cooking and cleaning and the services of a commissionaire. It was ideally located, too, with excellent horse-drawn bus services to most parts of central London, both along Baker Street and from nearby Oxford Street, an abundance of cabs and, of course, the newfangled Metropolitan Railway, the beginning of the great London Underground system, with a station at the Marylebone end of Baker Street. Not only would 221B Baker Street be convenient enough for Holmes both to continue his forensic studies and to travel about the city, but being in the West End it was also a more businesslike address and an easier one for his growing number of clients to reach.

As for Watson, it mattered little at this stage where he lived since the state of his health still prevented him from following his profession. All he needed was comfortable, independent accommodation that he could afford on his meagre income, with at least two good meals a day, so that he might gradually recover his strength. The Baker Street flat would have been affordable, in partnership with Holmes, in an area that offered plenty to interest a gentleman of leisure and within a few minutes' walk of Hyde Park, where he could take his exercise in extremely pleasant surroundings.

In the winter of 1880–1, of course, neither Holmes nor Watson was aware of how compatible their needs were. Holmes had already found the Baker Street flat and was looking for someone to share it, while Watson had been searching in vain for affordable rooms. It was entirely by accident that they came together, when Watson met a former colleague from Bart's Hospital and in the course of their conversation mentioned that he was looking for lodgings.

The scene of this meeting bears witness to Watson's somewhat cavalier attitude towards money and also his guilt about it. It took place in the Criterion, one of the most fashionable and expensive bars in London, where lunch would have cost at least twice the price that Watson would normally have paid. For a man who had already realized that he could not afford to continue living as he had been doing, it was an extravagant choice – but then it was New Year's Day 1881, and the doctor probably felt the need of some celebration. No doubt it was his conversation with his acquaintance Stamford that reminded Watson of his precarious financial position, and that was why the two men lunched not at the Criterion but at the more affordable Holborn Restaurant on their way to the meeting with Sherlock Holmes in the laboratory at Bart's.

The following day, as Watson recalls in the very first of his reminiscences, A *Study in Scarlet*, he and Holmes went to inspect the flat and 'the bargain was concluded on the spot, and we at once entered into possession'. Thus began one of the most enduring mysteries of the Sherlock Holmes stories: where exactly was, or indeed is, 221B Baker Street?

In 1881, Baker Street was a busy thoroughfare, as it is today, and in some ways its character was not all that different from its modern incarnation. The world-famous waxworks of Madame Tussaud were there at the time and there were dozens of shops, public houses and restaurants among the houses and mansion blocks. The Baker Street of Holmes's time was different in one important respect, however. It was much shorter than the present road.

Today, what is called Baker Street runs from the south-western corner of Regent's Park, across Marylebone Road and, on the western side, past Bickenhall Street, York Street, Crawford Street, Dorset Street, Blandford Street and George Street to Portman Square, at the

Baker Street today, an office block on the site of 221B

other side of which it becomes Orchard Street to the point where it meets Oxford Street. When Holmes and Watson lived there, though, Baker Street extended from Portman Square only as far as Crawford Street, after which the street was known as York Place until it reached Marylebone Road. This means that what was properly called Baker Street was about a third shorter than it is now, which in turn makes it impossible that there could have been a building numbered 221 at the time. In fact, the numbers listed for Baker Street in 1881 go no farther than 84. The obvious conclusion is that Watson was at pains in his memoirs to disguise the true address of Sherlock Holmes, as well he might have been in view of the risks his friend faced in his work, and as he certainly did for reasons of confidentiality with other significant addresses featuring in the stories.

So did Holmes actually live in York Place, which was the wholly residential end of what is now Baker Street, and did Watson rename the address so as to confuse those who might have wished Holmes harm and, equally, to make the location more immediately accessible to his readers? Could it be, otherwise, that Holmes and Watson actually lived at the Regent's Park end of the present-day

Baker Street, or what was then known as Upper Baker Street, on the northern side of Marylebone Road? Certainly, many people have thought so.

When Baker Street was extended across Marylebone Road and renumbered, the Abbey Road Building Society (which later became Abbey National) had its headquarters in the block covering what had become 219 to 229. This was only a few years after the publication of the very last Sherlock Holmes story and it was not long before the building society began to receive letters for the great detective addressed to 221B Baker Street – many of them seeking his help in solving some crime or mystery. So regular and voluminous did this correspondence become that the management of the building society was obliged to create the position of a posthumous secretary to Mr Sherlock Holmes.

Thus Abbey National could style itself as the official 'home' of Sherlock Holmes until, in 1990, the Sherlock Holmes Museum opened its doors at what it claimed was the 'real 221B', a house

The Sherlock Holmes Museum displays itself as 221B Baker Street.
In fact, this part of the street, north of Marylebone Road, was called Upper Baker Street in Holmes's day

with certain similarities to the one described in *A Study in Scarlet* (though the building was actually then numbered 239 Baker Street). A long dispute followed, with in 1994 the museum being refused permission to change its address to 221B. It retaliated by registering a business named 221B Limited, which allowed it to display the number at its entrance, much to the chagrin of local planning officials. In 2002 the Sherlock Holmes Museum found itself in an unchallenged position when Abbey National moved out of Baker Street – though not before sponsoring a statue of Holmes outside Baker Street Tube station. Thereafter the museum insisted that all the detective's correspondence be redirected to its own 221B.

However, the extension and renumbering of Baker Street did not take place until the 1930s. Back in 1881 the numbers of the houses in Upper Baker Street ran no farther than 54, so the theory that it contained Holmes's apartment suffers from the same objection as Baker Street itself. Are we, then, simply dealing with a change of number on Watson's part?

To be sure, there were several lodging houses in Upper Baker Street at the time. Most appear to have been run by maiden ladies, but at number 36 we find Mrs Sarah Ennis, so could she have been the real Mrs Hudson? As it turns out, this does not seem to be very likely. There is no indication that Holmes lived in an actual lodging house and no mention of any other tenants in his building. The only other people we hear about are Mrs Hudson the housekeeper and Peterson the commissionaire for the building (the latter replaced by Billy the page-boy in later years, presumably after the commissionaire's retirement). Nor is there any suggestion that Mrs Hudson is the actual owner of the property. Indeed, as will become apparent, Holmes and Watson almost certainly did not live in a lodging house – and a body of other evidence tends to dismiss the idea that he lived in Upper Baker Street at all, as well as the claims of both Abbey National and the Sherlock Holmes Museum.

The only way to discover the truth is to follow the clues, on the ground where necessary, given by Watson in his reminiscences. They lead to an inescapable conclusion.

An early pointer appears in the second story the doctor published, *The Sign of Four*, at the beginning of which Holmes gives Watson a demonstration of his powers by telling him that 'observation shows me that you have been to the Wigmore Street Post-Office this morning, but deduction lets me know that when there you dispatched a telegram'.

> 'Right,' said I. 'Right on both points. But I confess that I don't see how you arrived at it. It was a sudden impulse on my part, and I have mentioned it to no one.'
>
> 'It is simplicity itself,' he remarked, chuckling at my surprise – 'so absurdly simple that an explanation is superfluous; and yet it may serve to define the limits of observation and of deduction. Observation tells me that you have a little reddish mould adhering to your instep. Just opposite the Wigmore Street Office they have taken up the pavement and thrown up some earth, which lies in such a way that it is difficult to avoid treading in it in entering. The earth is of this peculiar reddish tint which is found, as far as I know, nowhere else in the neighbourhood.'

This is highly significant. Wigmore Street, where the site of the post office is still to be seen, runs from the south-east corner of Portman Square eastwards to Cavendish Square, effectively forming at its western extremity the end of both the modern and the Victorian Baker Street – though the portion immediately after Portman Square was originally known as Lower Seymour Street. The post office was just at the point where the name of the street changed, past the junction with Duke Street, which leads into Manchester Square. If we apply Sherlock Holmes's methods, this fact leads to the deduction that the real address hidden behind the fictional 221B must have lain firmly within the confines of the old Baker Street. Had the real address been Upper Baker Street, why would Watson have taken quite a long walk to Wigmore Street? Marylebone Road or Marylebone High Street would have offered post offices much closer to home, and that would also have been the case if 221B had been in York Place. Moreover, Holmes was evidently familiar enough with the condition of Wigmore Street to know that the pavement had been dug up, which clearly suggests that he often found himself there – much likelier if 221B was at that end of Baker Street.

There are further suggestions as to the location of 221B in the classic *The Hound of the Baskervilles*. After the visit to Baker Street by Sir Henry Baskerville and his friend Dr Mortimer:

> We heard the steps of our visitors descend the stair and the bang of the front door. In an instant Holmes had changed from the languid dreamer to the man of action.
>
> 'Your hat and boots, Watson, quick! Not a moment to lose!'
>
> He rushed into his room in his dressing-gown and was back again in a few seconds, in a frock-coat. We hurried together down the stairs and into the street. Dr Mortimer and Baskerville were still visible about two hundred yards ahead of us in the direction of Oxford Street … we followed into Oxford Street and so down Regent Street.

Sir Henry had refused Holmes's offer to call him a cab, saying that he preferred to walk back to his hotel, which was in Northumberland Street, leading from the southern edge of Trafalgar Square towards the river, along the side of Charing Cross Station. That would have been a long walk from the Marylebone end of Baker Street and, even if he had undertaken it, Sir Henry would not have walked the length of the road to Oxford Street. A much more direct route would have been via Paddington Street or one of the other side roads on the eastern side of Baker Street down to Marylebone Lane. From there he would have gone by Weymouth Street to Portland Place and on to Regent Street and Piccadilly Circus and finally across Trafalgar Square to Northumberland Street. It is true that Sir Henry himself, as a stranger to the city, would not have known of the shortcut, but Dr Mortimer, who had studied medicine in London and spent two years as a house surgeon at the Charing Cross Hospital, would surely have known where he was and would have guided Sir Henry towards the most direct route back to the hotel.

Again, the deduction must be that 221B was situated closer to Portman Square and Oxford Street than to the Crawford Street end of Baker Street.

The most compelling evidence for the precise location of 221B Baker Street, however, comes from the collection entitled *The*

George Street to the south and Broadstone Mews ran north to Dorset Street, it could only have been in those two blocks on the eastern side of Baker Street. But which block was it?

Here we must again follow the Holmes method. We have already deduced that the real 221B must have been towards the Portman Square/Oxford Street end of Baker Street and now we know that it lay on the western side of the street between George Street and Dorset Street, or in the blocks numbered at the time from 54 to 69 and from 70 to 78. In 1881 these two blocks were bisected by King Street, since renamed as the westward continuation of Blandford Street, which it was directly opposite. Holmes and Watson were in what was then the shorter Blandford Street, which ended at its junction with the east side of Baker Street.

Of the two narrow alleys off Blandford Street that Holmes could have used to reach the building facing 221B Baker Street, the

Now called Kendall Place, this is the mews off Blandford Street from which Holmes gained access to the so-called Camden House, opposite his rooms in Baker Street, where Colonel Sebastian Moran waited to shoot him with a powerful air-gun in 'The Empty House'

narrower one was Kendall Mews/Place. It was, and is, also considerably shorter than Broadstone Place/Blandford Mews, so it would have led more quickly to the empty house, in the way that Watson suggests. Also, there would have been less chance of the pair being spotted than if they had entered the rather more open and extensive mews on the northern side of Blandford Street. Furthermore, a Victorian map of the district shows that just a few steps from the entrance to Kendall Mews, almost in the middle of the row, was a single house with a yard, whereas off Blandford Mews the first place that could have matched Watson's description of Camden House was at least two hundred yards from the entrance to the mews.

Identifying this building today is quite difficult because of the enormous changes that have taken place in Baker Street, but what we can say with some certainty is that Watson's Camden House was more or less at the centre of the row of buildings on the eastern side of the street between George Street and Blandford Street. This leads to what seems to me to be an obvious conclusion. The real 221B was almost certainly number 75 Baker Street, directly opposite which Colonel Sebastian Moran had secreted himself in Camden House in order to take a shot with his highly accurate airgun through the window of Holmes's first-floor apartment.

The very fact that Watson placed a 'B' in the address confirms that, like many other buildings in that part of Baker Street at the time, there would have been a shop at street level and residential or office premises either above it or at the back. Given that Watson always refers to Holmes's visitors coming upstairs, the apartment was obviously on the first floor, above the shop.

We know that in 1880 the ground floor of number 75 was occupied by the stationer's business of Emile Mascart and that the rest of the building was residential, some of it at least occupied for a time by a Dr Mark Richardson. There is no mention of any Mrs Hudson at that address but then, given Watson's penchant for concealment, there can be little doubt that her name had been invented, too. Significantly, in 1905 the tenant of 75 Baker Street (Mascart the stationer was still there) is listed as Elaine Fowler, dressmaker – and by that time, of course, Holmes had retired to the country.

in London. Perhaps that was why he took an interest in a case which at first sight seemed hardly to warrant his expert attention.

'When I got back to my lodgings,' Miss Hunter told Holmes as she sought his advice about her new job, rather *in loco parentis*, 'I found little enough in the cupboard, and two or three bills upon the table.' At the time, around the turn of the century, Montague Place was remarkable in that, with the exception of a barrister, a vicar and a Member of Parliament named Jeremiah MacVeagh, its houses were occupied entirely by ladies managing lodging houses, private hotels or self-contained apartments. There was Miss Lucy Tucker at number 17 and next door Mrs Louisa Ellicott. Another Miss Lucy, with the surname Spooner, had a larger establishment at numbers 20 and 21. One can imagine that such places were filled with young women who, as Watson put it, had their own way to make in the world.

More recently, Montague Place was described as 'a forgotten part of London that has the potential to be one of the capital's great outdoor spaces' when featured in the 2008 London Festival of Architecture. 'An exciting temporary structure' 525 feet long was designed to provide 'new public spaces, a dramatic viewing gallery, outdoor exhibition spaces, lawned seating areas and performance spaces.' One doubts whether all that would have suited Miss Violet Hunter.

Still close to the British Museum, a more striking and easily identifiable relic of Holmes and Watson is to be found opposite in Great Russell Street. The Museum Tavern on the corner of Museum Street was the real name of the public house visited by Holmes and Watson as they pursued the case of 'The Blue Carbuncle', which we shall come across in a later chapter. Perhaps the most exciting location in Bloomsbury, though, is to be found on the northern side of Russell Square, off Woburn Place. This is the scene of 'The Adventure of the Red Circle', in which Mrs Warren of Great Orme Street consults Holmes about the bizarre behaviour of her lodger and a murder is later revealed.

Summoned urgently to the house after an attempt is made to kidnap Mrs Warren's husband in an apparent case of mistaken identity, Holmes and Watson find themselves outside 'a high, thin,

Russell Square, Bloomsbury, was and is a welcome green space close to Holmes's lodgings and would no doubt have been a place where he enjoyed relaxation from his studies at the nearby Pharmaceutical Society

yellow-brick edifice' in 'a narrow thoroughfare at the northeast side of the British Museum'. Great Orme Street is one of Watson's little fictions, so the first task is to find the real name of his narrow thoroughfare.

Working on the basis that the doctor is often quite literal in choosing his pseudonyms, the obvious candidate would be Great Ormond Street, which is indeed at the north-east side of the British Museum, albeit only slightly north. However, a number of factors work against Great Ormond Street. For one thing, it contained relatively few houses.

On the northern side of the road was the forerunner of the now world famous Great Ormond Street Hospital for Sick Children, which had been established there in 1852. A few years later the children's hospital was joined in Great Ormond Street by the London (now with the title Royal) Homoeopathic Hospital, which was expanding away from its original site in Golden Square, Soho.

Also on the north side of Great Ormond Street was the church of St John of Jerusalem, described at its opening in 1864 as 'a unique specimen of a pure Roman church in England', and next to it the hospital of St John and St Elizabeth, known today as 'John & Lizzie's' and situated in St John's Wood, to where it was moved stone by stone from its original location. Finally there was the Working Men's College, which had moved to Great Ormond Street from Red Lion Square in 1857 and had greatly expanded in pursuit of its mission to bring education to the working classes, teaching 'arithmetic, book-keeping, English grammar and language, history, literature, geography, physiology, Latin, French, German, drawing, singing, &c.' at evening classes for fees ranging from two to four shillings per class per term.

The other side of Great Ormond Street consisted mainly of commercial premises, though there was one lodging house owned by Mrs Mary Percival. What really counts against it, though, is the fact that there were no yellow-brick edifices in Great Ormond Street. Leading off it was, and still is, a whole row of them, beautifully preserved in Orde Hall Street, but they do not match other elements in the doctor's description of Mrs Warren's house.

If not Great Ormond Street, then where? A little farther north, again off Woburn Place, we find Coram Street, leading east to Brunswick Square, and in a late-Victorian edition of Stanford's Library Map of London we learn that it was then called Great Coram Street – quite literally a short step from the fictitious Great Orme Street. Further investigation will confirm the choice and lead us to a remarkable discovery.

The dropping of the 'Great' is far from the only change that has taken place in Coram Street and its surrounding area. Brunswick Square is now an architectural showpiece, an imaginative mix of shops, restaurants, apartments and a cinema. Next to it, the south side of Coram Street is taken up by a large hotel, the Holiday Inn, opposite which is a modern block of flats. Then, as we move towards Woburn Place, we come across a single 'high, thin, yellow-brick edifice' on the corner of what is now called Herbrand Street but was once Little Coram Street.

'Standing as it does near the corner of the street,' wrote Watson, 'it commands a view down Howe Street, with its more pretentious houses.' And so it does, though for Howe Street we must read Little Guilford Street on the Victorian map, while today we see it as the continuation of Herbrand Street.

This must surely have been the very house where, from the top-floor, Emilia Lucca watched Holmes and Watson walk down the modern Herbrand Street on their way to the discovery of the body of Black Gorgiano of the Red Circle:

> As we walked rapidly down Howe Street I glanced back at the building which we had left. There, dimly outlined at the top window, I could see the shadow of a woman's head, gazing tensely, rigidly, out into the night ...

CHAPTER THREE

Trains, Cabs and Shanks's Pony

TRAVEL ACROSS LONDON today and you have the choice of using your car – always assuming you are prepared to pay the Congestion Charge and can find one of the city's increasingly expensive parking places – or else one of the distinctive London taxis, a mini-cab, a 'bendy-bus' or the more traditional double-decker, the Underground, and, for the places the Tube cannot reach, a comprehensive railway network. Notwithstanding the inevitable problems of a crowded metropolis, free and rapid movement seems to us to be the essence of modern urban life and we can barely imagine functioning without it. What is easy to forget amid all our journeying is that, though the means of transport might have changed, the attitude was much the same in the days of Sherlock Holmes and Dr Watson and the details of travel round London are central to the doctor's memoirs.

London in Victorian times was for the age every bit as much a modern city as it is now and, in many ways, even more committed to development and progress. It was in London in 1863 that the first underground railway in the world was opened, a four-mile stretch carrying steam trains between Paddington and Farringdon Street Stations. Five years later, Westminster and Kensington were joined by Tube, in 1880 a tunnel from Tower Hill to Bermondsey was opened and by 1882 the Circle Line as we know its route today was complete. In 1890 the first deep-tunnel electrified service began, from the City to Stockwell, under the Thames, and the rest, as they say, is history. When Holmes and Watson moved into their apartment in Baker Street, the Metropolitan Line station at its northern end had been open for nearly twenty years and had even been equipped with new platforms offering services to Swiss Cottage and eventually to Aylesbury and beyond, a journey of some fifty miles.

It is not surprising, then, that by 1895, when Holmes investigated the case of the Bruce-Partington Plans, he was familiar enough with the London Underground to be able to work out how the body of a clerk from Woolwich Arsenal might have been transported to Aldgate Station, and from where – an event that will be described in more detail later.

'We will begin our investigation at Aldgate Station,' says Holmes, after hearing from his senior-civil-servant brother Mycroft that the loss of the plans placed the country in great danger. He, Watson and Inspector Lestrade of Scotland Yard must have walked along Baker Street to the Underground station and boarded a Circle Line train, for, 'an hour later, Holmes, Lestrade and I stood upon the Underground railroad at the point where it emerges from the tunnel immediately before Aldgate Station'.

Aldgate is in the City, of course, at the eastern end of Leadenhall Street. The Underground station is in Aldgate High Street and, as well as being on the Circle Line, at the time of the naval treaty case it provided services to Hammersmith and Richmond. Since the Second World War, when it was badly damaged by bombing, the station has also been the eastern terminus of the Metropolitan Line. It was close to Aldgate that on 7 July 2005 one of four deadly terrorist bombs was exploded on the Underground, on a Circle Line train from Liverpool Street.

In 1887, however, the Underground would not have been able to take Holmes and Watson directly from Aldgate to their next destination, London Bridge Station, from where they caught a train to Woolwich in order to look into the theft of secret papers that had brought about the murder of the clerk. Although it had been serving south-east London, Greenwich and Croydon since 1836, and had been extensively modernized and extended during the following years, London Bridge had no Underground connection until 1900, when a new branch of the Northern Line was built between the City and Kennington. What Holmes and Watson presumably did was continue on the Circle Line to Monument Station then walk down King William Street, where the Northern Line ended at that time, and across London Bridge to the mainline station.

Today there is little at London Bridge Station to recall its Victorian roots, except for a fragment of the old building at the western corner of Tooley Street. Redevelopment has continued after extensive rebuilding during the 1970s. At the time of writing, construction of what is promised to be the tallest skyscraper in western Europe is under way on the south-west side of the station, while the concourse itself is being further modernized to prepare for the arrival of the new Thameslink rail services. Yet the purpose of the station remains very much what it was in 1895, as a hub for rail services to south-east London and Kent – though a Victorian passenger would be astounded at the sheer number of people, 42 million, who pass through London Bridge each year.

It would have been fairly slow going for Holmes and Watson, just as it can be nowadays on stopping trains. They would have rattled through Bermondsey, Deptford, Greenwich, Charlton and Woolwich Dockyard before the train 'drew up at last' at what Watson calls simply 'Woolwich Station'. No doubt he meant Woolwich Arsenal Station, which, having first been opened in 1849, was to be rebuilt in London brick in 1906 and then completely remodelled into a circular steel-and-glass structure in 1996.

Having satisfied himself as to the circumstances of the theft of the papers and interviewed the clerk's fiancée, who had been with him on the fatal night, Holmes retraced with Watson the young man's journey back to London Bridge Station and we must assume that they then walked back across the bridge to Monument and returned to Baker Street on the Circle Line. Did he take the Tube again that day? Leaving Watson at home, he went out on 'a reconnaissance' and the next the doctor heard of him, 'shortly after nine o'clock', was from a messenger delivering a note that said Holmes was dining in Kensington. Given that he was searching for locations on the Underground, it must surely be the case that he travelled on the Circle Line to Gloucester Road Station, which was then officially known as Brompton (Gloucester Road) and continued to be so until 1907.

In 'The Adventure of the Bruce-Partington Plans' we have no actual proof of Tube travel and must merely assume that the Underground conveyed them to Aldgate. In 'The Red-headed League', on the other hand, Dr Watson acknowledges that 'we travelled by the Underground as far as Aldersgate'. That, too, would have been an easy journey on the Circle Line from Baker Street. The station was at the crossroads formed by Aldersgate Street, Long Lane and Barbican, from the last of which it took its modern name in 1968. It was to become notorious a few years after the case of the Red-headed League when it was the target of an Anarchist bomb and again in 1914 with the discovery in the ladies' cloakroom of the body of a little girl who had been sexually assaulted and suffocated. A display summarizing its history can be seen at the modern Barbican Station.

How often Holmes and Watson used the Underground (though in their day much of it actually ran above ground) is debatable, but we can assume that their use of it was fairly limited, given that it was not until the twentieth century that there really began the creation of the extensive network that now exists. They certainly made full use of main-line rail services, though, as evidenced by their regular consultations of Bradshaw's Railway Timetable in connection with out-of-town investigations. In fact the guide is mentioned by name only twice in the Holmes canon. Holmes himself refers to it in *The Valley of Fear*, remarking that 'the vocabulary of Bradshaw is nervous and terse, but limited' as he tries to identify the source of a coded message. In 'The Adventure of the Copper Beeches', when the governess Violet Hunter sends an urgent call for help from Winchester, Watson quickly finds the appropriate train by 'glancing over my Bradshaw'.

It is obvious, however, that the famous timetable would have been pressed into service many times as the pair journeyed throughout the country, since at more than nine hundred pages it was the only comprehensive guide to the multiplicity of companies then operating train services. As the magazine *Punch* once

three), and drive at a much quicker rate ... The driver's seat is at the back, so that he drives over the heads of the passengers sitting inside. Orders are communicated to him through a trap-door in the roof.

In 1899, normal cab fares for two people were one shilling for a journey of up to two miles and sixpence a mile thereafter, with a flat rate of sixpence charged for each additional passenger and twopence for large pieces of luggage. Cabs, however, were not obliged to accept fares wishing to travel more than six miles. Higher rates applied if they did and also for journeys outside a four-mile radius of Charing Cross, so that Holmes and Watson could easily have found themselves paying an hourly rate of up to two shillings and sixpence for a hansom. That might explain why they seem often to have favoured four-wheelers, which were rather less expensive.

'Some of the London cabmen are apt to be insolent and extortionate,' Baedeker warned its readers. 'The traveller, therefore, in his own and the general interest, should resist all attempts at overcharging, and should, in the case of persistency, demand the cabman's number, or order him to drive to the nearest police court or station.'

There is no record of Holmes and Watson ever encountering such difficulties, partly because Holmes took care to maintain contacts among the cabmen, who could supply him with information, but also because he seems to have been unfailingly generous to drivers who accepted his sometimes demanding hirings.

We have already followed the circuitous journeyings by four-wheeler in *The Sign of Four*, but, apart from the original trip from Baker Street to the Lyceum Theatre, there would have been no cost involved because one driver was employed by Thaddeus Sholto and others by the police. Similarly, the fare would not have been much of a factor in Dr Watson's curious trip from his home to Victoria in 'The Final Problem', which I mentioned earlier.

Holmes's instructions were clear:

Now listen! You will dispatch whatever luggage you intend to take by trusty messenger unaddressed to Victoria to-night. In the morning you will send for a hansom, desiring your man to take neither the first nor the second which may present itself. Into this hansom you will jump,

*and you will drive to the Strand end of the Lowther Arcade, handing
the address to the cabman upon a slip of paper, with a request that he
will not throw it away. Have your fare ready, and the instant that
your cab stops, dash through the Arcade, timing yourself to reach the
other side at a quarter-past nine.*

All this, of course, was designed to throw Moriarty's agents off the
scent. Holmes suspected that they would be watching Watson and
he did not want to give them any opportunity to follow him. The
choice of the Lowther Arcade as a focal point was a good one. Built
in the 1830s on the model of a covered Oriental bazaar, the arcade
was described by George Augustus Sala in 1859 as 'a tube of shops
running from St Martin's Churchyard into the Strand, very nearly
opposite Hungerford Market'.

In his book *Gaslight and Daylight*, Sala, a journalist and social
commentator, observed:

*This tube is light and airy, and roofed with glass … it is resonant with
the pattering of feet, the humming of voices, the laughter of children,
the rustling of silken dresses, and buying, selling, bargaining and chaf-
fering. The commodities vended in the Lowther Arcade I may classify
under three heads: Toys, Jewellery, and Minor Utilities.*

There follow several hundred almost poetical words about the joys
of shopping in this shrine of mid-Victorian consumerism but, given
that by the 1890s it was somewhat run-down and catering for, shall
we say, the lower end of the market, it was hardly the sort of place
to which a respectable doctor would rush in a hansom.

Today the toyshops and jewellers have gone and the place is no
longer an arcade, but the attractive building in which the arcade
was housed is still there, opposite Charing Cross Station, itself
built in the 1860s on the site of the Hungerford Market referred to
by Sala. Interestingly, one of the occupants of the block that
contained the arcade is the famous Coutts Bank, which under
various names has been in the Strand since 1692 and moved into
the Lowther Arcade building when the arcade was demolished and
the whole block was modernized in 1904.

This elegant building at the western end of the Strand, opposite Charing Cross Station, once housed the famous Lowther Arcade, through which Dr Watson dashed to throw any of Professor Moriarty's agents off his trail as he went to join Holmes at Victoria Station in 'The Final Problem'

Back in 1891, Dr Watson followed Holmes's instructions to the letter and drove immediately after breakfast to the Strand entrance of the Lowther Arcade, 'through which I hurried at the top of my speed'. At the other side he found not a hansom or a four-wheeler but a brougham, a closed four-wheeled coach with a glazed front window, perhaps the closest Victorian equivalent of the small family car. It was only later that the doctor discovered his driver had been Holmes's brother Mycroft, who had presumably obtained the coach from the government vehicle pool.

As soon as he stepped into the brougham the driver 'whipped up the horse and rattled off to Victoria Station'. They must have set off along Whitehall to Parliament Square and turned left into Victoria Street, which would have been the shortest route. There was obviously no question of a fare and as soon as Watson stepped out of the coach the driver 'turned the carriage and dashed away again without so much as a look in my direction'.

A fare would have applied, though, to the strange cab ride taken by Holmes and Watson in 'The Empty House', the sequel to 'The Final Problem', in which, as we saw in Chapter 2, the detective supposedly killed at the Reichenbach Falls dramatically reappeared in London. We followed them on foot along Holmes's tortuous route from Cavendish Square to Baker Street, but we can now describe the equally serpentine journey that brought them in a hansom from Kensington.

'I had imagined that we were bound for Baker Street,' wrote Watson, but he must have been still suffering from shock at his friend's sudden resurrection or else he would surely have queried the instructions Holmes must have been shouting to the driver through the trapdoor in the roof.

Assuming that they set off from Watson's home in Kensington, the location of which will be suggested in Chapter 6, the quickest way to Baker Street would have been up Kensington Church Street to Notting Hill Gate and from there straight along the Bayswater Road and Oxford Street. That would not have suited Holmes's purpose, however, since he was anxious that none of the survivors of the Moriarty organization should follow him. Nor, in the event that someone was observing them, would it have made much sense to pass the end of Baker Street and continue along Oxford Street to Cavendish Square – and Watson would surely have questioned it if Holmes had indeed taken that route, since it was at Baker Street that he was expecting to arrive.

What Holmes must have done if he seriously intended to throw off potential pursuers was to set off along Kensington High Street towards Knightsbridge, pass the southern end of Hyde Park and go via Piccadilly to turn left and head north along Bond Street. At the top of Bond Street they would have crossed Oxford Street into Henrietta Street, in which they would then have turned right and arrived, as Watson noted, at the corner of Cavendish Square, from where they could follow on foot what was 'certainly a singular route' back to Baker Street. On the other hand, Holmes might simply have demanded to be taken to Cavendish Square and the driver, as cabbies all over the world are sometimes inclined to do, might simply have decided to go the long way round.

So far we have trailed our heroes as they used means of transport that are familiar enough to Londoners today. The Underground might be electrified and hugely more extensive, the main-line trains might no longer be steam driven and the cabs might be powered by diesel engines rather than horses, but the theory and practice of mass transit in the city are fundamentally the same as they were in the nineteenth century. One element, however, is missing from the Watsonian travelogues – the great London bus. There is no record of Holmes and Watson ever having boarded an omnibus, in spite of the fact that Baker Street was served by or close to quite a few of the one hundred and fifty or so routes that crisscrossed London. Indeed, given the number of times they took trains, one might think that they would have sometimes used the special services provided by the railway companies to connect to the main stations for a flat fare of about 3 pence or free for passengers holding train tickets.

It was not as if there was anything particularly new and strange about the London bus services. The first was started in 1829 by George Shilibeer, who had been introduced to the idea while working in Paris a decade earlier. The Shilibeer bus ran from the Yorkshire Stingo pub in Paddington, along what is now called Marylebone Road then via Euston Road, Pentonville Road and City Road to Bank junction. Pulled by three horses, the green bus carried twenty-two passengers, who were provided with newspapers, magazines and books and paid a shilling for the full journey.

Before long the 'Shilibeers', as the early buses were popularly known, covered much of London but, as public transport expanded rapidly during the 1830s, they faced well-financed competition from other companies, including the Post Office, and their creator was eventually forced out of business. Within a few years, bus services were dominated by two large concerns, the London General Omnibus Co. and the London Road Car Co., the first of which had also diversified into trams. By the 1890s, LGOC alone operated 1,300 buses with 15,000 horses and 500 drivers and conductors.

In those days there were no designated bus stops. Passengers simply hailed the bus they wanted in the street, as with cabs. The Baedeker Guide to London that appeared in 1899 noted:

> *The destination of each vehicle (familiarly known as a 'bus), and the names of the principal streets through which it passes, are usually painted on the outside. As they always keep to the left in driving along the street, the intending passenger should walk on that side for the purpose of hailing one. To prevent mistakes, he had better mention his destination to the conductor before entering ... The vehicles have been considerably improved of late years; the 'garden seats' on the top are pleasant enough in fine weather and are freely patronized by ladies.*

Fares varied from a halfpenny to sixpence or sevenpence depending on the journey and the route.

It may be that Holmes and Watson were usually in too much of a hurry to rely on buses, which can be as true today as it was then in spite of the introduction of special bus lanes on the roads, but I suspect that there was also a certain class-consciousness involved. Holmes was in the habit of travelling first class on trains and we have seen Watson complaining bitterly about Josiah Amberley's insistence on third class for their outing to Essex. Holmes was evidently far from being a snob. There are several cases in which he appears to have viewed members of the upper classes with a degree of distaste and he lost no opportunity for pricking pomposity and deflating self-importance. He could be kind and gentle with less elevated clients and he seems to have enjoyed friendly relations with street arabs and members of the criminal classes, but none of that would mean he would have been happy to rub shoulders with hoi polloi on a London omnibus. As for Watson, though he was a generous and amiable character, he shared with many Victorian gentlemen a high degree of sensitivity in relation to his dignity and social position and neither of these would have been well served by travelling in the 'garden seat'.

When the speed, privacy and relative comfort of a hansom or four-wheeler were not required, rather than taking a bus Holmes and Watson tended to make their journeys on foot. They were evidently enthusiastic and regular walkers, often spending their

CHAPTER FOUR

Going East

ONE OF THE best-known quotations in the Sherlock Holmes canon occurs towards the end of the story 'Silver Blaze', in which Holmes is invited by Inspector Gregory to investigate the apparent murder of a racehorse trainer and the disappearance of the eponymous favourite to win the Wessex Cup. Holmes solves the mystery within hours but, with his customary love of theatricality, insists on stage-managing the denouement, while offering the police detective a few cryptic clues. The inspector asks if there is any point to which Holmes wishes to draw his attention and receives the reply:

> 'To the curious incident of the dog in the night-time.'
> 'The dog did nothing in the night-time.'
> 'That was the curious incident,' remarked Sherlock Holmes.

There is a similar curiosity attached to the activities of the most successful and celebrated detective in London and his relationship to the City and East End of the capital.

The City of London during the Victorian age was awash with financial fraud and scandal, particularly in connection with speculative investment proposals and company flotations of the sort practised by the 'gigantic swindler' Augustus Melmotte in Anthony Trollope's acerbic novel *The Way We Live Now*. The 1880s and 1890s were the great days of the likes of the dubious company promoter Ernest Terah Hooley, who made personal profits of a staggering £7 million in two years from a sort of pyramid scheme of flotations then went bankrupt and served two prison terms for fraud. Yet there is no record of Holmes having ever investigated any such crimes, which could and certainly often did lead to the ruin of thousands of people. This in spite of the fact that his arch-enemy Professor Moriarty – the 'Napoleon of crime' and 'the organizer of half that is evil and of nearly all that is undetected' would undoubtedly have had some involvement in such lucrative criminal endeavours.

It was not that Holmes never came into contact with elements of the most important financial centre in the world. The client in the case of 'The Beryl Coronet' was none other than Alexander Holder, the senior partner of the banking firm Holder and Stevenson, of Threadneedle Street, 'the second largest private banking concern in the City of London'. The crime in question, however, was associated with finance only in the sense that Mr Holder had made a loan of £50,000 against the deposit of 'one of the most precious public possessions of the empire', part of which was subsequently stolen by the banker's niece and her aristocratic cad of a lover. It was not Threadneedle Street but Mr Holder's home in Streatham that became the centre of the affair, as we shall see later when we follow Holmes and Watson into the suburbs.

Similarly, although 'New Zealand stock, paying 4½ per cent' to Miss Mary Sutherland, is crucial to 'A Case of Identity', and her stepfather Mr Windibank operates his dastardly plot to entrap her from the post office in Leadenhall Street while working as a clerk at a wine importers in Fenchurch Street, the City is a mere bit-player in the drama.

'I dare say E.C. is not much in your line,' remarks Holmes's ambitious young client Hall Pycroft, from the firm of Mawson and Williams in Lombard Street, in 'The Stock-broker's Clerk'. On the evidence presented by the cases Watson chose to publish, it is hard to disagree with that assessment.

The only time Dr Watson mentions that Holmes had actually set foot in the City comes in 'The Mazarin Stone', when the detective follows the villainous Count Negretto Sylvius to the workshop

many a crisis. Cold grey eyes, looking shrewdly out from under bris-
tling brows, surveyed each of us in turn. He bowed in perfunctory
fashion … I understood not only the fears and dislike of his manager
but also the execrations which so many business rivals have heaped
upon his head.

Holmes, for his part, displayed no more warmth towards a man
distraught at the apparent murder of his wife and the arrest of the
young woman he really loved. Had his heart not been touched by
the desperate situation of the wronged Miss Dunbar – 'brunette,
tall, with a noble figure and commanding presence, but … the
appealing, helpless expression of the hunted creature' – it is clear
that he would not have persisted with the investigation. He
certainly treated Mr Gibson with something less than respect on
their first meeting in Baker Street: 'I am a busy man, Mr Gibson,
and I have no time or taste for aimless conversations. I wish you
good-morning … You have a good deal yet to learn.'

The City, its denizens and its crimes, then, were not especially
appealing to Holmes. The closest he came to a case in the Square
Mile was the planned bank robbery in 'The Red-headed League'.

This is one of Dr Watson's most famous memoirs, but it is also
perhaps one of the best disguised from the point of view of its location. The premises of the pawnbroker Mr Jabez Wilson are recorded
as being in Saxe-Coburg Square, Clerkenwell. Watson recalls it as
being on the City side of Clerkenwell and places it not far from
what he terms Farrington Street – obviously a slip of the pen for
Farringdon Street, which was and still is the continuation of
Farringdon Road, running south from Holborn Viaduct to Ludgate
Circus at the end of Fleet Street. A further, though vague, piece of
identification is given when Holmes and Watson visit Saxe-Coburg
Square for the first time, reaching it according to the doctor after a
short walk from what was then Aldersgate Underground Station.

In 1890, when the events described took place, there was no
square in Clerkenwell, or anywhere else in London for that matter,
called Saxe-Coburg. The name given to it by Watson is obviously
fictitious, no doubt to protect the bank from which the pawnbroker's new assistant had planned to steal a large quantity of gold.

There were, however, four squares close to Aldersgate Station, so could it have been in one of these that the plot was hatched?

This part of London has benefited from (or suffered, depending on one's point of view) very extensive modern redevelopment, not least the construction of the vast bulk of the Barbican Centre, with its smart apartments, arts centre and restaurants, which now replaces the road from which its name was taken. Two of the nineteenth-century squares near Aldersgate Street have disappeared under the tower blocks and raised walkways, so any connection with Mr Jabez Wilson and the City and Suburban Bank is impossible to verify with complete accuracy.

Falcon Square, lying to the south of Aldersgate Station towards London Wall, would certainly have been as seedy as the one indicated

The towers and high walkways of the Barbican now cover two of the squares that might have been Dr Watson's model for the Saxe-Coburg Square in Clerkenwell that features in 'The Red-headed League'

by Watson. It would also have been an easy walk from there to Fleet Street for Mr Wilson when he was inveigled into taking his position with the Red-headed League. What counts against it is the fact that it was in the City proper, rather than the City side of Clerkenwell, though its position as given by Watson might have been nothing more than an understandable fault of geography.

Another possible setting might have been Nicholl Square, a little closer to the station, but unless Watson's imagination overwhelmed him it seems unlikely, since it abutted a large cattle market, a fact the doctor would hardly have failed to mention. That, too, now forms part of the foundations of the Barbican. A further candidate that turns out to be improbable is the third square that lay within easy reach of Aldersgate Station. This is Charterhouse Square, which still exists today, but it is altogether too grand for the somewhat depressing place Holmes and Watson encountered.

In the midst of the Barbican development, Bridgewater Square remains where it was in Victorian times and could have been the basis of Watson's description of the non-existent Saxe-Coburg Square, where Jabez Wilson had his shop in 'The Red-headed League'

The closest model for Watson's description of Saxe-Coburg Square was probably Bridgewater Square, reached from Beech Street, a few hundred yards east of Aldersgate Station. Amazingly, it has survived redevelopment and provides a welcome open space after the tunnel formed by the so-called Barbican High Walk that is the modern incarnation of Beech Street. It is certainly a short walk from the station, which of course has been renamed Barbican but continues to be served by the Circle and Metropolitan Lines, just as it was when Holmes and Watson travelled there. Nothing remains of the former character of the square, though, apart from the small garden at its centre, which gives it a direct association with Saxe-Coburg Square. This had, at its heart, 'a small railed-in enclosure, where a lawn of weedy grass and a few clumps of faded laurel bushes made a hard fight against a smoke-laden and uncongenial atmosphere', as Watson put it. Today the garden in Bridgewater Square is well kept and pleasant, full of adventurous playthings used by the children from a nursery school.

On the other hand, the Victorian Bridgewater Square was not quite a match for Watson's description of Saxe-Coburg Square. It might well have looked run-down and uncongenial, as a centre of the fashion accessories trade, with a furrier, some milliners and a collection of ostrich-feather makers, small businesses that would not have been wealthy, but there is no record of a pawnbroker and there was no bank nearby into which 'the murderer, thief, smasher and forger' John Clay could have tunnelled, at least not without some serious engineering. There was a branch of the London and County Bank, one of the forerunners of NatWest, in Aldersgate Street, close to the station but, in order to reach it from Bridgewater Square, Clay would have had to negotiate the foundations of several large buildings, including the extensive local workhouse, and get under the main road, too.

That is not to say, however, that Bridgewater Square could not have served as Watson's geographical disguise. I suspect that he might have taken the characteristics of the real scene of the attempted crime and simply superimposed them on somewhere else. The London and County Bank, for instance, which he and Holmes would have seen as they came out of Aldersgate Station –

it is still there, as a branch of NatWest – might well have suggested the name 'City and Suburban' as a disguise for the bank he was describing. As usual, the good doctor sprinkles his narrative with a few clues.

There might not have been a Saxe-Coburg Square in Clerkenwell, but there was a Coburg Street. Situated north and west of Aldersgate Street, it ran from Meredith Street to Skinner Street and, even though it was not a square, it contained a number of elements that might associate it with the case of the Red-headed League. There was a pawnbroking establishment in the neighbourhood, and nearby in St John Street – characterized correctly by Watson as 'one of the main arteries which carried the traffic of the city north and west' – might be found the models for 'Mortimer's the tobacconist' (actually Thomas Jarman) and 'The Vegetarian Restaurant' (possibly John Rock's dining-rooms, opposite Spencer Street). Unfortunately there is no record of a carriage-building depot in the area, so what prompted Watson to draw attention to one called MacFarlane's is unknown. Perhaps he was simply trying to put his readers off the scent by altering the function of one of the many small manufacturing enterprises in the neighbourhood.

If it was Coburg Street that Watson converted into Saxe-Coburg Square, where was the bank that prompted John Clay and his accomplice to invent the Red-headed League in order to tempt Jabez Wilson out of his shop so as to leave Clay free to dig his tunnel? In nearby St John Street were to be found building societies and Post Office savings banks, but they were unlikely to have taken delivery of the £30,000 worth of gold napoleons that attracted the robbers. Just off St John Street, however, and a few hundred yards south of Coburg Street, was the Finsbury and City of London Savings Bank, its solid and quietly substantial building still in existence today at the northern end of Sekforde Street. Could this, then, have been the real 'City and Suburban Bank' of Watson's memoir?

For this to be the case, John Clay would have had to have built quite a long tunnel from Coburg Street, under Meredith Street and Corporation Row, in order to reach the bank. This would not have been entirely impossible, even though Jabez Wilson told Holmes that his absences from his shop during his engagement with the Red-headed League lasted no more than eight weeks. In fact, other details in the memoir suggest that the would-be bank robber could have had much longer to complete his work.

Watson is not always very good with dates and this can lead to serious contradictions in his accounts of cases. Here he tells us that the advertisement for the Red-headed League in *The Morning Chronicle* appeared on 27 April 1890, 'just two months ago', as he says he commented at the time. He must have misremembered, though, because the notice on the door of the League's offices announcing its dissolution was posted not eight weeks later but, according to Watson's own account, on 9 October. Assuming that these dates are correct, young Clay would have had not two months but five for the purpose of digging his tunnel. In view of the fact that he was known to Holmes and the police as a daring and determined criminal, he might well have undertaken such a huge task with £30,000 at stake. Such an impression is reinforced by the information from the bank director Mr Merryweather that the gold had been sitting in the bank's vaults for 'some months', not some weeks, at least time enough for the bank to receive 'several warnings that an attempt might be made on it'.

What is beyond doubt is that it would have been considerably easier for young John Clay to tunnel into the Finsbury and City Savings Bank from somewhere near Coburg Street than it would have been for him to reach the London and County Bank from Bridgewater Square.

Yet it could be that Watson was indulging in a sort of double-bluff. If the Finsbury and City Bank was the real location of the attempted robbery he might well have sought to disguise it by taking the name of a nearby street, applying it to one of the streets closer to the bank and, in a further piece of obfuscation, turning it into a square. There were several pawnshops in the area, some in streets closer to the bank – Corporation Row or Woodbridge Street, for example. Both of these were close to Coburg Street and backed on to the Finsbury and City building and would therefore

Watson called it Pope's Court, but he might have been thinking of Mitre Court, at the western end of Fleet Street, when he described the place where Jabez Wilson copied the *Encyclopaedia Britannica* in 'The Red-headed League'

We cannot leave this story without remarking upon one curiosity. This is the false forwarding address given by Duncan Ross when he abruptly dissolved the Red-headed League: 17 King Edward Street, near St Paul's. This was a real street, still to be seen today though changed beyond recognition. It runs from Newgate Street, north of the cathedral, to Little Britain, Montague Street and the western end of London Wall. Not only did Watson see no reason for disguising this location, since it was peripheral to his story, but it would have held fond memories for him because it runs alongside St Bartholomew's Hospital, where he had studied and had eventually met Sherlock Holmes. Perhaps it was memories of his carefree days as a medical student that prompted Watson to indulge in a little humour at the expense of a man for whom he evidently felt a certain class-conscious contempt.

According to him, Jabez Wilson told Holmes that when he visited the forwarding address given by the man he knew as Mr Ross, to inquire about the closing of the league, he found the building occupied by a manufacturer of artificial kneecaps. We can say with certainty that, during the 1880s, numbers 16 and 17 King Edward Street were occupied by Messrs Dalton, Barton & Co. Limited, 'manufacturers of carriage lace &c'. By 1900 those numbers had vanished, subsumed into a large building occupied by the General Post Office. Watson must have been simply taking the mickey out of the self-important and, in the doctor's eyes, rather vulgar Mr Wilson. His assessment of the man is clear:

> Our visitor bore every mark of being an average, commonplace British tradesman, obese, pompous and slow. He wore rather baggy grey shepherd's check trousers, a not over-clean black frock-coat, unbuttoned in the front, and a drab waistcoat with a heavy brassy Albert chain, and a square pierced bit of metal dangling down as an ornament. A frayed top-hat and a faded brown overcoat with a wrinkled velvet collar lay upon a chair beside him.

If cases in the City were not really to Holmes's taste, there is little evidence that he was any more attracted to the East End, where 'like the enormous black, motionless, giant Kraken, the poverty of London lies in lurking silence and encircles with its mighty tentacles the life and wealth of the City and of the West End', as a writer put it in 1891. Parts of the East End in Holmes's day formed a malodorous sink of crime, with some districts so lawless and violent during the 1880s that the police never entered them.

It was the districts of Aldgate, Bethnal Green, Bow, Limehouse, Mile End, Poplar, Stepney, Shadwell and Whitechapel, with their grim poverty and desperate overcrowding, that provided the model for the Victorian London immortalized by Charles Dickens and were described in terms of horror and pity by many social-reforming writers such as Charles Booth, Jack London and George Bernard Shaw. In the 1880s a Russian Jewish immigrant to Whitechapel asked plaintively: 'Was this London? Never in Russia, never later in the worst slums of New York, were we to see such poverty.' Destitution forced many men and children into *which has been of value – that highest value which anticipates and prevents rather than avenges crime.'*

Holmes would not have been keen for Watson to broadcast such aspects of his always unorthodox methods, certainly not in view of the increasingly eminent clients who sought his advice, either in person or through their agents, or of the developing profession-alism of the police.

Whether Porlock and Shinwell Johnson were actual denizens of the East End, and how Holmes encountered them, is not revealed, but the atmosphere of the meeting between Holmes and Johnson recorded by Watson in 'The Illustrious Client' is strongly suggestive. Asked by Holmes to look into the activities of the murderous Baron Gruner in an effort to prevent his marriage to the daughter of General de Merville, Johnson produces Miss Kitty Winter, a woman from the evil baron's past. She displays the characteristics of an East End girl no-better-than-she-should-be who had seen her chance to escape when the baron picked her up.

'It seems,' writes Watson, 'that he had dived down into what was peculiarly his kingdom.' Miss Winter tells them: 'I'm easy to find. Hell, London, gets me every time. Same address for Porky Shinwell.' The lustful and brutal Gruner with his book of sexual conquests was just the sort of man who would have frequented the teeming alleys of the East End in search of loose women. Furthermore, the fact that Kitty Winter took her revenge on her destroyer by throwing acid in his face offers a strong indication that she had grown up seeing such punishment meted out, which suggests her origins might have been in the world of violent gangsters.

A likely East End gang known to Holmes appears in 'The Adventure of the Three Gables', employed to retrieve from an old lady a manuscript written by her late son that incriminates the wealthy and unscrupulous Isadora Klein. Watson introduces the case in dramatic fashion with a threatening visit to Baker Street by 'the bruiser' Steve Dixie, 'one of the Spencer John gang', who is implicated in 'the killing of young Perkins outside the Holborn

Bar'. Again, though, it is not in Limehouse, Bethnal Green or Stepney that Holmes encounters other members of the gang, but in peaceful and respectable Harrow Weald.

That Holmes did conduct a successful investigation among the 'vile alleys' in 1895 is recorded in 'The Adventure of Black Peter', when Watson refers to 'his arrest of Wilson the notorious canary-trainer, which removed a plague-spot from the East End of London'. Those are all the details we are given, however, and there has been much speculation about the nature of the case.

We do find Holmes and Watson actually in Stepney as part of their wide-ranging search for 'The Six Napoleons', which we shall explore further in the chapter that deals with Kensington (Chapter 6). The doctor is sparing in his description of the area, preferring instead to locate it by means of the journey:

> In rapid succession we passed through the fringe of fashionable London, hotel London, theatrical London, literary London, commercial London, and, finally, maritime London, till we came to a riverside city of a hundred thousand souls, where the tenement houses swelter and reek with the outcasts of Europe. Here, in a broad thoroughfare, once the abode of wealthy City merchants, we found the sculpture works for which we searched.

This broad thoroughfare was almost certainly Mile End Road, where little or nothing of the once great houses that made up the 'Millionaires' Row' of London is to be found among the blocks of council flats, ethnic restaurants and little shops close to Stepney Green. Even by 1900, when it is generally agreed this investigation took place, the seriously wealthy were long gone from Mile End Road and it was well established as the home of countless commercial establishments, as it is today.

Among the tradespeople there at the beginning of the twentieth century were numbers of small workshops offering gilding, picture-framing, carving and similar types of artisanship, so it would have been entirely natural to find the sculpture works of Gelder & Co. in the neighbourhood. The German manager and Italian workforce would also have been typical, since for centuries the district had been home to various waves of immigrants from Europe, as Watson pointed out.

Another rare foray into the mysterious East comes with the case of 'The Man with the Twisted Lip', when Watson is dispatched to an opium den by the Thames to rescue a friend who has fallen victim to addiction. We are back in the year 1889, shortly after Watson's marriage, and it is his friend's wife who persuades him to visit the Bar of Gold in Upper Swandam Lane, where he finds a disguised Sherlock Holmes engaged on 'a very remarkable inquiry'.

Mr Neville St Clair, 'a gentleman who appeared to have plenty of money', has disappeared and the fear of his wife is that he might have been done to death in the Bar of Gold. But what was such a man – 'of temperate habits, a good husband, a very affectionate father' – doing in an opium den? And what do the bloodstains on the frame of the window overlooking the river mean?

It is in this memoir that we are perhaps closest to the seamy side:

Upper Swandam Lane is a vile alley lurking behind the high wharves which line the north side of the river to the east of London Bridge. Between a slop-shop and a gin-shop, approached by a steep flight of steps leading down to a black gap like the mouth of a cave ... I made my way into a long, low room, thick and heavy with the brown opium smoke, and terraced with wooden berths ...

There was no shortage of gin-shops in the neighbourhood and doubt-less there were not a few opium dens. The slop-shops would have enjoyed brisk trade, too. 'Slops' was the derogatory name given to cheap, ready-made clothing of the sort probably sold by Thompson and Llewellyn the tailors in St Mary-at-Hill, a lane running from Lower Thames Street north to Little Tower Street. This was an area frequented by sailors, fishermen bringing their catches to Billingsgate market and merchant seamen whose vessels landed tea, coffee and exotic fruits from the Indies and China, or coal from the north-east of England, or wine from France and Portugal.

It was a teeming district of narrow lanes and even narrower alleys, presided over by the Custom House at the eastern end of Lower Thames Street and the ancient church of St Magnus the

The church of St Magnus the Martyr, in Lower Thames Street, is one of the very few landmarks Holmes and Watson would recognize today if they were able to revisit the scene of 'The Man with the Twisted Lip', near London Bridge

Martyr close to London Bridge. Between the two were shipping agents, importers, maritime insurance brokers, wharfingers, boat and barge builders and literally hundreds of fish merchants trading in everything from oysters to herring. Among them were dozens of taverns and liquor shops, coffee-houses and purveyors of the opium that was a by-product of the China trade. Fights were frequent, murders not uncommon. This was dangerous territory into which Neville St Clair had strayed, followed by Holmes and later Dr Watson – though Holmes had evidently been there before.

'Briefly, Watson, I am in the midst of a very remarkable inquiry, and I have hoped to find a clue in the incoherent ramblings of these sots, as I have done before now. Had I been recognized in that den my life would not have been worth an hour's purchase; for I have used it

before now for my own purposes, and the rascally lascar who runs it has sworn to have vengeance upon me. There is a trap-door at the back of that building, near the corner of Paul's Wharf, which could tell some strange tales of what has passed through it on moonless nights.'

Although the area retained many of its riverside characteristics until late in the twentieth century – for instance, whitebait were still being landed just west of Tower Bridge as recently as the 1950s – there is now almost nothing to connect it with its past, apart from river buses and sightseeing cruisers. The only ship visible is the museum vessel HMS *Belfast*, moored impotently by the southern bank east of London Bridge. On the northern side, the vast pile of the Custom House remains and is still used as the headquarters of the Customs Service, but the Billingsgate market hall now functions only as a venue for corporate events, since the fish market was transferred to a site close to Canary Wharf in the new Docklands development in 1982. The twelfth-century church of St Magnus has also survived, though it is isolated and all but invisible among the vulgar glass and steel corporate head-quarters and other office buildings that line both sides of Lower Thames Street.

The dingy, dangerous alleys that Holmes and Watson knew – and the real location of Upper Swandam Lane – are merely distant memories. Perhaps it was Harp Lane, or Beer Lane, or Water Lane. There we would have found the Old Ship tavern and Mrs Sarah Owen's dining-rooms, the commission agent Jacob Grundelfinger and the Harp Inn. Could the Bar of Gold have been in one of their cellars? It would not, of course, be listed in the Post Office London Street Directory. Or else it was the alley that joined them all, running behind the wharves at the riverside. It cannot have been Love Lane, one of the few of its kind that can still be seen (though renamed Lovat Lane) because we know that the window of the opium den opened on to the river and Love Lane ends on the north side of Lower Thames Street.

Nor do other clues contained in the narrative offer much help, because Watson is dissembling again:

Lovat Lane, east of London Bridge, is one of the few surviving alleys in this part of the City that recall the 'Upper Swandam Lane' Watson describes as the location of the opium den in 'The Man with the Twisted Lip'

'Last Monday Mr Neville St Clair went into town rather earlier than usual … Now, by the merest chance, his wife received a telegram upon this same Monday, very shortly after his departure, to the effect that a small parcel of considerable value was waiting for her at the offices of the Aberdeen Shipping Company. Now, if you are well up in your London, you will know that the office of the company is in Fresno Street, which branches out of Upper Swandam Lane …'

According to Holmes's account, as reported by Watson, it was as she walked along Upper Swandam Lane that Mrs St Clair caught sight of her husband, apparently in some distress, at a window in the Bar of Gold and it was that, coupled with his subsequent disappearance, that caused her to raise the alarm. The doctor, however, is up to his old trick of mixing fact and fiction here. The Aberdeen Shipping Company was real enough, if we presume that he meant the Aberdeen Steam Shipping Company, but its offices were actually in Old Bailey, quite some distance from London Bridge, and its cargoes were received at the company's wharf at the bottom of the now disappeared Emmett Street in Poplar, beyond Tower Bridge and a very long way east of the supposed location of the Bar of Gold. Of Fresno Street I have discovered no trace.

What is easier to find is the source of the name Upper Swandam Lane. Immediately west of London Bridge, on the other side of the historic Fishmongers Hall, is a short street running down to the river called Swan Lane. One might think that Watson simply moved this eastward and disguised it by taking the 'Upper' from Thames Street – or else that he just made a mistake in locating it to the east of the bridge. This cannot have been the case, however. In the 1880s, though there was a tavern in Swan Lane, much of the lane was taken up by a school, which was hardly likely to have had an opium den in its basement. The other three buildings in the street seem equally improbable locations: a chandler's shop, Henry Watts's dining-rooms and the premises of a painter and glazier. Nor did Swan Lane go all the way down to the river. It joined Old Swan Lane, which gave access to Swan Pier, and this was completely occupied by busy commercial warehouses. There was not a gin-shop or a slop-shop in sight.

If all the old lanes have disappeared, it is at least still possible to follow the Thames Walk from London Bridge to Tower Bridge, past the ghostly remains of the old wharves, the dockside cranes and the steps leading down to what were once moorings for the lighters. There we can, with a little imagination, evoke at least to some degree the atmosphere of Upper Swandam Lane in 1889. Today, it is all as respectable as Mr Neville St Clair, whose only misdemeanour was to be unmasked as a failed actor who had made his fortune posing as a disfigured beggar in the City and who was in the habit of applying his costume and make-up at the opium den.

CHAPTER FIVE

South of the River

IF THE EAST END was familiar but little visited territory for Sherlock Holmes, at least in the annals of Dr Watson, the same is not true of areas south of the Thames that were also known to harbour dangerous criminals. These southern parts feature in quite a number of the investigations chronicled by Watson, from virtually all stages of his friend's career.

The earliest example we can pinpoint of Holmes's interest in what he was inclined to call 'the Surrey side' arises from a comment in 'The Adventure of the Illustrious Client', when Holmes remarks in connection with the villainous Baron Gruner's expertise in Chinese ceramics that all great criminals have complex minds. 'My old friend Charlie Peace,' he adds, 'was a violin virtuoso.'

That was indeed the case. Charlie Peace was an infamous – one might almost say celebrated – Victorian cat burglar whose reputation was as ambiguous as that of the highwaymen of the previous century, and he was a violinist of some talent. In fact, when he moved to London from his customary haunts in Yorkshire, he set himself up as a dealer in musical instruments in Stangate Street, Lambeth, while he spent every night burgling properties in Camberwell and other parts of south London. Later he took the leases on neighbouring houses in Billingsgate Street, Greenwich, and persuaded his wife and son to move from Hull to join him, then after a short time they all took up residence in Evelina Road, Peckham.

Thus settled, Peace embarked on a wave of burglaries in Streatham, Denmark Hill and Blackheath, sometimes travelling to work in a pony and trap and carrying his house-breaking tools in his violin case. Quite when Holmes got to know him is uncertain, but it must have been at the very beginning of his days as a private detective, for Charlie Peace was arrested during a burglary in Blackheath in 1878 and hanged the following year for murdering some time earlier the husband of a woman with whom he had been having an affair. His one-man crime spree in south London lasted only two years, beginning in 1876, at about the same time as the young Sherlock Holmes was taking up residence in Montague Street, Bloomsbury.

We know from Watson's account that although the young Holmes continued to study during his early days in London, he had actually begun to act on behalf of clients while still at university, so it is possible that he got to know Charlie Peace while supporting himself as 'a consulting detective' in order to finance the completion of his studies.

'Even when you knew me first, I had already established a considerable, though not very lucrative connection,' Holmes told Watson in 'The Musgrave Ritual'.

He is certain to have been in contact with others of his profession, of whom there were many in Victorian London – he undoubtedly knew 'my friend and rival Barker', as we learn in 'The Adventure of the Retired Colourman' – and he might even have been called in to help investigate the burglary epidemic south of the river in 1878.

Perhaps, too, it was the suburban nature of south London in those days that produced not only crimes of particular interest to Holmes but also many of the sort of clients most likely to consult him: often solid, respectable people who felt their security threatened or else had become involved in tragic or apparently inexplicable events.

That was indeed the situation confronting Miss Mary Sutherland, the victim of 'A Case of Identity', who lived with her mother and stepfather at 31 Lyon Place, Camberwell. She was the very model of suburban lower-middle-class respectability in her slate-coloured, broad-brimmed straw hat, with a feather of a brickish red; her black beaded jacket, dark brown dress with purple plush at the neck and sleeves; her worn greyish gloves and her jet jewellery. She had an income of £100 a year from a small inheritance in addition to her wage as a typist. Thus, at a time when, as Holmes pointed out, a single lady could get on very nicely upon an income of about £60, Miss Sutherland had both the means and the confidence to engage a private investigator to solve the mystery of her fiancé's disappearance on the very day they were to be married.

This case did not require Holmes to travel to Camberwell, since he was able to deduce from his armchair that Miss Sutherland's stepfather had impersonated the man who had proposed marriage to her in order to get his hands on her inheritance. That being so, we have no means of establishing the location of Lyon Place. All we can do is assume that it was not too far from a railway station, either Denmark Hill or, more probably, Loughborough Junction, since the stepfather, Mr Windibank, commuted to work in the City and trains from the latter would have taken him directly there.

Camberwell crops up again, though only as an aside, in the introduction to one of the cases that followed Watson's marriage, 'The Five Orange Pips'. Remarking upon how busy Holmes was during 1887, the doctor mentions the Camberwell poisoning case, in which 'Sherlock Holmes was able, by winding up the dead man's watch, to prove that it had been wound up two hours before, and that the deceased had gone to bed within that time – a deduction which was of the greatest importance in clearing up the case'.

The only time we actually find Holmes and Watson on the ground in Camberwell (apart from the doctor's visits to Mary Morstan) is during one of the chases in *The Sign of Four*, as we saw in Chapter 1. Similarly, although the source of the goose in 'The Blue Carbuncle' is identified as the home of Mrs Oakshott at 117 Brixton Road, Holmes did not find it necessary to pay her a visit, having obtained the information he needed from the Covent Garden dealer we met earlier.

For 'The Adventure of the Veiled Lodger', we are taken to what Holmes identifies loosely as South Brixton to visit the former circus wife, Eugenia Ronder, horribly disfigured after being attacked by a lion. Watson describes the house in some detail – it circular one-way traffic system, with a small park where the graveyard used to be.

If the criminals were indeed planning to bury Lady Frances at St Matthew's, why did they feel the need to go as far as Kennington Road to find an undertaker, rather than using one closer to hand? The answer lies in their own explanation to Holmes, when he arrived at the house in Trinity Square and insisted on viewing the body placed in the coffin that had been delivered. It was not that of Lady Frances, but of a very old woman:

'Well, if you really must know,' Peters told Holmes and Watson, 'she is an old nurse of my wife's, Rose Spender by name, whom we found in Brixton Workhouse Infirmary.'

In fact, the workhouse that served Brixton was in Lambeth, occupying with its infirmary a vast site between Renfrew Road and Holyoak Road, off Kennington Lane. Of course, Peters was lying when he told Holmes the old woman had been his wife's nurse. To begin with, the woman he was with was not his wife and even if she had

The Master's House – all that remains of the Brixton Workhouse where the kidnappers of Lady Frances Carfax obtained the old woman's body that was intended to cover up a murder

been it is unlikely that she would ever have had a nurse. The couple had obviously just claimed a body from the Lambeth Workhouse Infirmary and would no doubt have been advised to make arrangements for the funeral at the undertaker the workhouse usually dealt with – the closest, at the nearby junction of Kennington Road and Reedworth Street, a mere three streets away from the workhouse.

Mr Ashton would have welcomed their business. Most of his work would have been for paupers, so that when a specially built coffin was ordered (to accommodate Lady Frances as well as the old woman), there would have been every incentive to please the client. It was the fact that 'it took longer, being out of the ordinary', which alerted Holmes to Peters's plan to dispose of Lady Frances and allowed Holmes to rescue her at the very last moment.

If we place the date of the crime in 1902, which seems the more likely, Ashton the undertaker, as I indicated earlier, would no longer have existed and the only such service in Kennington Road would have been offered by James Dadley, at number 345, between Lower Kennington Lane and Milverton Street. That, however, would still have been close enough for Mr Dadley to have been engaged by the workhouse when the need arose, which would have led the potential murderers of Lady Frances Carfax to his door.

Today, Lambeth Workhouse is but a memory, like another institution close to Kennington Road, the Bethlehem Royal Hospital for the insane, popularly known as Bedlam, which is now the site of the Imperial War Museum. Most of the workhouse complex had been reduced to rubble when I visited it, part of a large-scale redevelopment scheme, but the former Master's House was still there, containing an annexe of the Maudsley Hospital and a cinema museum.

With 'The Adventure of the Six Napoleons', we are again in Kennington Road, where the principal consulting rooms of the well-known Dr Barnicot could have been one of several medical establishments of the period – about 1900 – listed in the Post Office London Street Directory. There was one at number 75, on the east side close to the junction of Lambeth Road; another at 133; a large practice, almost a clinic, between Ship Lane and Wincott Street, which might well have been Dr Barnicot's, since position: then, as now, it was a busy thoroughfare and lined with commercial premises – jewellers, outfitters, coal merchants, a brewery, several hotels and public houses and the famous Barkers department store. There was a veterinary surgery and an optician, but not a single doctor because the accommodation available was largely unsuitable. Kensington Road, leading from the High Street to Hyde Park Gate, was more residential, containing on its south side the homes of MPs, generals, genteel ladies and minor members of the aristocracy. Much the same was true of the side roads, such as Vere Gardens and Kensington Court, though a surgeon is listed as living in a rather grand house close to Hyde Park Gate. This does not seem like the territory of the solid and respectable but unpretentious Dr Watson.

Perhaps, then, he had settled in the more northerly and perhaps slightly less grand – though only slightly – quarter of Kensington, situated on the north side of the High Street and eventually merging with Notting Hill. An indication of this might lie in the details of Holmes's theatrical unmasking of himself in Watson's study.

Disguised as an elderly bookseller, Holmes had literally bumped into his old friend outside the house in Park Lane where Ronald Adair had been murdered and had followed him home.

'I am a neighbour of yours,' he explained to the bemused doctor, 'for you'll find my little bookshop at the corner of Church Street.'

The corner he referred to is unlikely to have been at the junction of Kensington High Street because of the nature of the buildings there, so what Holmes was indicating was almost certainly that his shop was at the corner of Church Street and one of the roads leading off it, where a variety of little shops can still be found. Bearing in mind access to Kensington Gardens, this leads me towards the view that Dr Watson's house might well have been in Vicarage Gate, sitting between Church Street and the gardens and at the time leading directly into them.

Since he was a childless widower, Watson would probably not have occupied the whole of one of the substantial, four-storey houses running back to back along the northern and southern legs of the Gate. My assumption is that, together with the maid he

Vicarage Gate, Kensington, where Watson must have lived following the death of his wife and where Holmes made his dramatic 'return from the dead' in the case of 'The Empty House'

mentions and probably a cook/housekeeper, he occupied what would have been a large apartment taking up perhaps part of the ground floor and basement of one of these attractive buildings, its pillared portico offering his patients a dignified and reassuring entrance to his consulting room.

There were at the time maiden ladies living in Vicarage Gardens who might well have found it convenient to let part of their large houses to a respectable widowed doctor. We know from the records, for example, that parts of number 17 Vicarage Gate were at one time let to an architect and a surveyor, so the practice in the then relatively new houses was not unusual.

Arriving home in time for tea on that pleasant April afternoon, Watson would subsequently have found no difficulty in strolling past the vicarage and St Paul's Church into Kensington Gardens, striking north-east into Hyde Park and eventually reaching the house in Park Lane that was the object of his interest. It would have been a walk of perhaps twenty minutes or half an hour.

Kensington Gardens, though technically part of the former royal hunting ground that became Hyde Park, had been separated from it on the orders of Queen Caroline, wife of George II, in 1728 – presumably because of the proximity of that part of the park to Kensington Palace. At the same time, the Queen commissioned the first real landscaping work in the park, which included the provision of the stretch of water that became known as The Serpentine. Hyde Park was the site of the Great Exhibition of 1851, of which the centrepiece was the architect Joseph Paxton's Crystal Palace, later moved to Sydenham Hill in south London.

On the eastern side of Hyde Park, Watson's destination, Park Lane, where the Honourable Ronald Adair had been murdered, was, in the words of a Victorian estate agent's brochure, one of the most recherché addresses in London, 'enjoying the Varied Scenery of the Park, the distant Hills of Surrey, and the salubrious Air therefrom, while at the same time it is placed in the Centre of Fashion'. That was a long way from its origins as a narrow, rutted and often muddy turnpike running down the side of Hyde Park, from which it was separated by a high brick wall. In the 1740s Park Lane was characterized in an official report as one of a number of thoroughfares which had 'by reason of the many Carriages, frequently passing through the same, become very ruinous, and many Parts thereof are, in the Winter and wet Seasons, so bad that the same are dangerous to Passengers'. It was not until the 1820s that significant improvements began to be made and, following demands from the residents of the large houses that had been built, the wall of Hyde Park was demolished and replaced by iron railings. Another fifty years would pass, however, before the first signs of the wide avenue we see now began to appear and it was not until the period following the First World War that Park Lane started to acquire its modern features. Today, of course, this wide avenue is best known for its collection of luxury hotels: the Dorchester, the Grosvenor House, the Hilton, and so on.

Watson has Ronald Adair living at number 427, but this did not exist. Park Lane had been renumbered in 1871, but those numbers went no higher than 140. Since the higher numbers were at the Oxford Street end, we must assume that it was in that part where

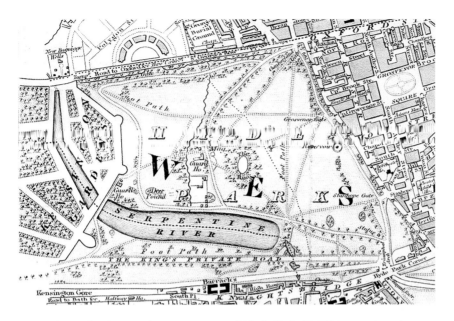

An early nineteenth-century map of Hyde Park. Dr Watson enjoyed walks through the park and was occasionally able to persuade Holmes to accompany him

Watson found what must have been a reasonably large house 'separated from the street by a low wall and railing'. Ronald, second son, as we are told, of the Earl of Maynooth, was in good company, though by 1894 Park Lane was already acquiring what some criticized as a flashy, nouveau riche quality. The soap manufacturer William Hesketh Lever (later Viscount Leverhulme) and the newspaper baron Edward Levy-Lawson lived in the neighbourhood, as did the financier James Hall Renton – not to mention the scandalous author Frank Harris. Nevertheless, the aristocracy was still well represented at the time, even if its presence was diminishing. The heir to the Duke of Devonshire lived at number 117, the politician Lord Tweedmouth at Brook House, the Dowager Countess Grosvenor and her second husband at number 99, Viscount Clifden at 93 and Viscount Molesworth at 98. The Hon. Ronald would have had no difficulty moving in 'the best society', as Watson put it, and 'a narrow and conventional circle'.

It was here, as he was trying to deduce how the murder might district would not match Watson's description of the one he visited. My suspicion is that Mr Culverton Smith, who was actually a resident of Sumatra, was not listed in the Post Office Directory, which permitted the cautious doctor to falsify his address. What he called Lower Burke Street might well have served for Lower Addison Gardens, which leads off Holland Road to the west of Holland Park, and is an area that does indeed contain some fine houses of the sort portrayed by Watson.

A similar sort of deception characterizes another Kensington neighbourhood that captured Watson's pen, this time on the borders of what is now usually thought of as Earls Court. It occurs in 'The Adventure of the Bruce-Partington Plans' when Holmes set out to discover how the body of the young Woolwich Arsenal clerk Arthur Cadogan West came to fall from a Metropolitan Railway train at Aldgate Station. Holmes had already obtained from his brother Mycroft a list of the addresses of three foreign spies who might be involved in the theft of the secret plans from Woolwich and when he located those addresses on a map, his attention was directed towards what Watson called Caulfield Gardens, Kensington, near Gloucester Road. There, at number 13, lived a notorious agent named Hugo Oberstein, who was reported to have been in London on the night of Cadogan West's death but to have left the city shortly afterwards.

Holmes – though not Watson at this stage – realized the significance of this Kensington address. It was the only one of those associated with the spies that was close to a Metropolitan and District Railways station, Gloucester Road. Moreover, one of the railway lines running through Gloucester Road Station was the Inner Circle, the same line that served Aldgate, as it still does today. That, together with Oberstein's sudden departure, seemed to Holmes's acute intellect to be more than a coincidence and he began to outline to himself a possible or even probable scenario.

The absence of blood at the place where the body had been discovered on the railway line at Aldgate, and the fact that no train ticket had been found on the victim, suggested that the clerk had not actually been killed on the train – that had merely been used to transport his body from elsewhere. But how?

Gloucester Road Underground Station, with its Metropolitan and District Railway façade. It was from here that Holmes tracked the killer in 'The Bruce-Partington Plans'

Holmes had remembered noticing during his frequent forays on the train that along the western stretch of what was then known as the Inner Circle Line 'the Underground runs clear of tunnels at some points', as he later told his friend. With that in mind, Holmes made his way to Gloucester Road Station and persuaded 'a very helpful official' to escort him along the track until he found what he was looking for – an open stretch of the line with houses backing on to it. This was by what Watson recorded as Caulfield Gardens, where not only did the back-stair windows open on to the line but also 'owing to the intersection of one of the larger railways, the Underground trains are frequently held motionless for some minutes at that very spot'. It must have been there that poor West's body had been dumped on the roof of a Metropolitan train, where it had remained until the points at Aldgate had dislodged it.

With such detail available, it should be easy to follow in Holmes's footsteps to the scene of the crime in Caulfield Gardens, the next generation, but Holmes obviously wondered whether grand opera of the grandest sort was really to Watson's taste.

Incidentally, this reference casts doubt on Watson's recollection of the dates of *The Hound of the Baskervilles* case. The year was almost certainly 1889, on the basis of other dates given in the narrative, but Watson must have been mistaken about the season. He places it in the autumn but it could in fact only have taken place in the spring. The Covent Garden seasons in which *Les Huguenots* was presented with the De Reszkes for several years during this period ran from May to July.

Amid all the accurate reportage on Watson's part there is one mystery which bears upon one of our surviving London locations. In the early part of 'The Adventure of Retired Colourman', Holmes suggests that they set the mystery on one side for a time: 'Carina sings to-night at the Albert Hall, and we still have time to dress, dine, and enjoy.' But who was Carina? I have been unable to find a record of any contemporary singer of that name, so it must be that Holmes was simply using the Italian adjective carina, meaning 'dear' or 'darling' or 'charming', as an affectionate and respectful nickname for a female performer well known to both of them.

It has been suggested that he might have been referring to the villainess-heroine of 'A Scandal in Bohemia', Irene Adler, a noted contralto of whom Watson wrote: 'To Sherlock Holmes she is always *the* woman. I have seldom heard him mention her under any other name. In his eyes she eclipses and predominates the whole of her sex.' Miss Adler, it will be remembered, outwitted Holmes in the matter of compromising letters and a photograph sent to her by the King of Bohemia. He was so impressed by her that after her escape he asked the king for her photograph, prompting Watson to repeat: 'And when he speaks of Irene Adler, or when he refers to her photograph, it is always under the honourable title of *the* woman.'

Miss Adler had clearly built quite a reputation for herself among opera lovers, as Holmes discovered when he looked up her name in his legendary index: 'Born in New Jersey in the year 1858. Contralto – hum! La Scala, hum! Prima donna Imperial Opera of

Warsaw – yes! Retired from the operatic stage – ha!' Strange that as a music lover he appears not to have heard of her before, but perhaps her fame had been confined to the United States and the Continent.

That is the first reason to doubt that Holmes could have spoken of Irene Adler as carina. There are other reasons, too, that weigh against the idea. The first is a simple matter of dates. The problem of the King of Bohemia was presented to him in 1888 and it was a full ten years later that Holmes made his remark about the singer who was appearing at the Albert Hall. It seems unlikely that distance would have lent enchantment to the extent that Holmes would have employed such a term of endearment. Second, in Watson's account of the case he quotes Holmes as saying that Irene Adler had already retired from the opera and settled in London, so she would hardly have been singing in concert a decade later. What clinches the matter, however, is that when Watson published his recollections of the case he referred to 'the late Irene Adler, of dubious and questionable memory', so that she could absolutely not have been singing at the time of 'The Adventure of the Retired Colourman' in 1898.

A more plausible theory, advanced by dedicated Italian students of Holmesiana, is that the singer Holmes referred to as 'Carina' was actually the celebrated Adelina Patti, who did indeed appear in concert at the Albert Hall in July 1898, having retired from her appearances in operas. The great Patti was known round the world by a series of affectionate nicknames, including La Divina, and there is every chance that Carina was among them. Our scholars might be going a little too far in suggesting that Adelina Patti was actually a friend of Holmes and Watson, but it seems to me there is a convincing case for her being the singer the pair went to see that evening at the Albert Hall.

One interesting feature of Holmes's musical excursions is that they seem almost always to have involved some time in a restaurant on the way, suggesting that his appreciation of good music was matched by his enjoyment of good food, or else that he thought Watson could only survive hours of listening to the classics on a full stomach. Italian cooking appears to have been a particular favourite of Holmes. 'Might I trouble you to be ready in half an hour, and we can stop at Marcini's for a little dinner on the way?' he asked Watson, for example, when suggesting that he might like to see the De Reszke brothers in *Les Huguenots* at Covent Garden. Then, preparing to bring about the denouement in 'The Adventure of the Bruce-Partington Plans', he summons Watson to join him at 'Goldini's Restaurant, Gloucester Road, Kensington' and to bring with him 'a jemmy, a dark lantern, a chisel and a revolver' in order to effect Holmes's plan to trap the criminal.

I have found no trace of Goldini's, which Watson described as 'garish', as well he might, being a respectable British gentleman ill at ease with Italian enthusiasm. No doubt he did not wish to afford the real establishment undue publicity, which is probably why he also placed it in another street, since there appears to have been no Italian restaurant in Gloucester Road at the time, though there might well have been such eating places in the area, as there are today. In Gloucester Road we now find Il Borgo and the long-established Da Mario, which advertises itself as treating its customers to 'Gastronomia Napoletana' and as having numbered among its clients the late Diana Princess of Wales and her children.

Similarly, the true identity of Marcini's is obscure, though since it was on the way from Baker Street to Covent Garden we might find it in Soho – perhaps Molinari at the Hotel d'Italie in Old Compton Street, where two shillings or so would have bought one an excellent table d'hôte dinner – or else in the Strand, where Gatti's restaurant was recommended for its reasonable prices. Holmes and Watson both enjoyed good food, but it is hard to see either of them being happy to pay inflated gourmet prices. That would explain why the celebrated Criterion in Piccadilly Circus does not appear after Watson's meeting there with his friend Stamford that led to his introduction to Holmes. The Criterion, which opened in 1874, was one of the most expensive restaurants in London, with dinner costing from five shillings up to half a sovereign (ten shillings), depending on the room in which it was served. Still on its original site, and with its luxurious Byzantine interior of marble, mosaic and gold fully restored, the Criterion is today part of the Marco Pierre White group, though its modern menu is more *brasserie* than the self-consciously *haute cuisine* of old.

On the other hand, there is the example of another of London's world-famous restaurants, the Café Royal, at the southern end of Regent Street near Piccadilly Circus. In 'The Adventure of the Illustrious Client', Watson reads in the evening paper:

> *'We learn with regret that Mr Sherlock Holmes, the well-known private detective, was the victim this morning of a murderous assault … the event seems to have occurred about twelve o'clock in Regent Street, outside the Café Royal … The miscreants who attacked him appear to have been respectably dressed men, who escaped from the bystanders by passing through the Café Royal and out into Glasshouse Street behind it.'*

What, we might ask, was Holmes doing at the Café Royal at the time of day when he was attacked by the thugs of the infamous Baron Gruner he was pursuing if he was not going for lunch? This was 1902, by which time Holmes had long been a celebrity, had received a variety of native and foreign honours and lavish gifts, and was presumably enjoying an income sufficient for a five-shilling French meal, plus a fee for attendance and a *couvert* of up to a shilling.

Yet there are objections to this idea. In those days, 'lunch' was something portable, say bread and cheese, carried by working men who lived too far from their jobs to be able to return home for dinner, while 'luncheon' was either a generally light meal served to the residents of the best houses – most often to women and children while the husband was engaged in his business – or else a slightly more substantial affair available to people staying in hotels. Our modern idea of lunch was gradually gaining popularity, but it was still not common in most of the best restaurants, including the Café Royal, for a midday meal to be served.

As Baedeker's London guide was explaining as late as 1900: 'The dinner hour at the best restaurants is 4–8 p.m., after which some of them are closed. At less pretentious establishments dinner "from the joint" is obtainable from 12 to 1 or 5 to 6 p.m. Dinner from the

Joint is a plain meal of meat, potatoes, vegetables and cheese.' Such 'luncheon bars' as there were could be found mainly in the City, serving the people who worked there and charging between sixpence and eightpence 'for a chop or a small plate of hot meat with bread and vegetables', according to Baedeker. Otherwise it was possible to obtain luncheon in some taverns or at one of the many gentlemen's clubs of the period, if one was a member. With the dinner hour beginning at four o'clock, many people still saw no need to have a significant meal in the middle of the day, particularly when they had partaken of a leisurely and substantial breakfast. Holmes and Watson certainly liked to start their days with a satisfying meal. An indication of this comes at the end of 'The Naval Treaty', when Holmes offers his client Percy Phelps a choice of breakfast dishes:

> 'Mrs Hudson has risen to the occasion,' said Holmes, uncovering a dish of curried chicken. 'Her cuisine is a little limited, but she has as good an idea of breakfast as a Scotchwoman. What have you there, Watson?'
>
> 'Ham and eggs,' I answered.
>
> 'Good! What are you going to take, Mr Phelps: curried fowl, eggs, or will you help yourself?'

Curried leftovers of chicken was a popular breakfast dish at the time and Mrs Hudson had no doubt taken the recipe from Isabella Beeton who, incidentally, in 1880 reinforced the traditional idea that dinner was the 'grand solid meal of the day'. The chances are, then, that when Holmes was outside the Café Royal at twelve o'clock he was merely passing by on his way elsewhere when he was attacked.

In any case, the Café Royal was hardly Holmes's style. Founded in 1865 by a fleeing French bankrupt, it went on to become a hub of highly fashionable and sometimes raffish social life, frequented by the likes of Oscar Wilde and Frank Harris and their circles. It continued to be a magnet for royalty, leading politicians, celebrities and socialites for more than a century. Today, still on its original site at 68 Regent Street and comprehensively restored, it is a partner establishment of the hotel Le Méridien Piccadilly and used for conferences and events.

More suited to the tastes, and the pockets, of Holmes and Watson was another still-surviving and even more venerable star of the London culinary firmament, Simpson's in the Strand. This splendid and quintessentially British restaurant features at the end of 'The Adventure of the Dying Detective' when Holmes, having feigned being near death in order to trap the dastardly Mr Culverton Smith, remarks: 'When we have finished at the police-station I think that something nutritious at Simpson's would not be out of place.' Nutritious their dinner certainly would have been, and at half the price of the Café Royal.

Simpson's began as the Grand Cigar Divan in 1828, established by Samuel Reiss on the site of the old Fountain Tavern, which had been the home of the legendary Kit-Kat Club that featured Addison

Simpson's in the Strand. This splendid and essentially British restaurant was an evident favourite with Holmes and Watson

He deceived Watson again, of course, in the character of the elderly Italian priest which he adopted in order to escape the attentions of Moriarty in 'The Final Problem'. With such talent at his disposal, he would have no doubt considered it boring to watch other, possibly less skilful, exponents of the art.

Watson, by contrast, seems to have been just the sort of chap who would have relished a good drama, or perhaps even more an entertaining comedy. He must surely have attended the Gaiety, the Vaudeville, the Lyceum or the Haymarket during the weeks of idleness at his private hotel in the Strand that followed his return from India. However, he does not record many of the interests and activities he pursued without Holmes or with either of his two wives. All we are permitted to know about is his fondness for the Turkish baths that once existed at Nevill's in Northumberland Street, to which he later introduced Holmes.

It is these baths, opened in a specially constructed large building a few yards from the Thames in 1884, that cause some debate as to the date of the case of Lady Frances Carfax, as I mentioned earlier. Watson begins his reminiscence by relating an exchange between Holmes and himself:

> 'But why Turkish?' asked Mr Sherlock Holmes, gazing fixedly at my boots. I was reclining in a cane-backed chair at the moment, and my protruded feet had attracted his ever-active attention.
>
> 'English,' I answered in some surprise. 'I got them at Latimer's, in Oxford Street.'
>
> Holmes smiled with an expression of weary patience.
>
> 'The bath!' he said; 'the bath! Why the relaxing and expensive Turkish rather than the invigorating home-made article?'
>
> 'Because for the last few days I have been feeling rheumatic and old. A Turkish bath is what we call an alternative in medicine – a fresh starting-point, a cleanser for the system.'

Watson clearly believed that the expense that Holmes referred to was worth it. Nevill's in Northumberland Street (and at its branch at New Broad Street in the City) charged considerably higher prices than any of its competitors. A 'plain hot-air bath with shower' cost a princely three shillings and sixpence, a full shilling more than, say, Culverton's in Argyll Place, near Oxford Circus. The cost would be even higher if the client desired perfumed vapour, scented showers and a spinal douche. For that money, however, a bather could relax in some luxury. In the hot rooms, the floors were covered with marble mosaic, the ceilings with enamelled iron, and there was much decorative use of ceramics and stained glass. There was marble seating and, in the cooling-rooms and smoking-rooms, there were upholstered divans. One can see that it might appeal to the rheumaticky Watson.

How Holmes deduced that the doctor had been to the Turkish baths from the condition of his boots will be explained later. For the moment we shall merely compare that conversation with a statement made by Watson as he introduces 'The Adventure of the Illustrious Client':

> Both Holmes and I had a weakness for the Turkish bath. It was over a smoke in the pleasant lassitude of the drying-room that I found him less reticent and more human than anywhere else. On the upper floor of the Northumberland Avenue establishment there is an isolated corner where two couches lie side by side, and it was on these that we lay upon September 3, 1902, the day when my narrative begins.

That dates the case with absolute precision, so we can assume that the investigation into the disappearance of Frances Carfax was earlier, given that Holmes's attitude towards expensive Turkish baths had apparently changed in the meantime. How much earlier is the question. While some Holmes devotees have placed the gap at some years, others have suggested that it was just a matter of months and that it was actually Watson's visit to Nevill's before the earlier case that had presented him with the opportunity to convert his friend to this particular Oriental pleasure as a means of relaxation and to persuade him to try it.

So we have concert halls, opera houses, restaurants and Turkish baths, but the London theatres do not figure greatly in Dr Watson's memoirs.

We find the Lyceum, of course, in *The Sign of Four*, but only as in luxury hotels. The deluxe new Linley suites are to die for. Claridge's Bar is one of Mayfair's, indeed London's, hottest spots. Don't miss "Gordon Ramsay at Claridge's" restaurant or the award-winning afternoon tea.' The 'Gold King' would certainly feel quite at home there if he were to take a suite today.

Similarly, the Langham Hotel is still at its original home in Portland Place, where it welcomed the Hon. Philip Green, would-be lover of Lady Frances Carfax, in 1902. Though he was 'the son of a famous admiral of that name who commanded the Sea of Azof fleet in the Crimean War' (which means that the name Watson had given him was obviously fictitious), Green evidently lacked the means of a J. Neil Gibson.

The Langham had opened in 1865 as the first grand hotel in Europe, attracting on its first day 2,000 visitors come to gawp and marvel at its magnificence. It also drew a fair selection of the wealthy, aristocratic and even royal, but as the century progressed it faced increasing competition from hotels such as the Savoy, the Cecil near Waterloo Bridge and later the Carlton, at the corner of Haymarket and Pall Mall, and Claridge's. In 1900, when the minimum room price at Claridge's was ten shillings, the Langham was charging just four shillings and sixpence. It was the sort of place where Philip Green could afford to spend some time, having returned from South Africa with no family home in London open to him.

In later years, the Langham was to become famous as a sort of annexe to the headquarters of the BBC across the square, Broadcasting House, while its glamour seemed to have declined somewhat. By the time it celebrated its 140th anniversary in 2005, however, a £50 million programme of refurbishment was under way with the intention of restoring the vast hotel's former greatness, and a couple of years later it felt justified in charging just under £5,000 a night for its premium Infinity Suite.

Both the Langham and Claridge's were identified by Watson as a means of indicating the status of their occupants with whom Holmes was concerned. It was something he began when the thought first occurred to him that some accessible record of his friend's remarkable abilities should appear and he produced A Study in Scarlet. To communicate something of the character of the villain Enoch J. Drebber, the doctor saw fit to record that he had taken lodgings in distinctly insalubrious Camberwell (in the Torquay Terrace that I failed to find during my researches south of the river) and also that he had another bolthole in Euston, at Halliday's private hotel.

For whatever reason, Watson chose to withhold the true identities of both these places, and I have had no more success in uncovering Halliday's than I had in attempting to reveal the correct address of Madame Charpentier's lodging house in Camberwell, where Drebber also stayed. We are told the private hotel was in Little George Street, to the west of Euston Square, but at the time of the investigation there were no hotels in that street or in those that intersected it. There was, however, just such a place run by Mrs Mary Emms at 56 Drummond Street, only a few hundred yards from Little George Street and in those days a main road running past the front of the station and the famous Euston Arch. The arch was demolished amid a great deal of controversy in the 1960s to make way for London's first Inter-City railway station, something of a marvel at the time, and in the process half of Drummond Street disappeared. That means no trace remains of the building that was once Mrs Emms's hotel, which was just a few doors west of the arch, but it does seem likely that this was the actual establishment Drebber used. Watson must have changed the name and the location so as not to embarrass the respectable lady owner, while at the same time letting his readers know that the foul, drunken Drebber had balked at staying at one of the 'proper' hotels near the station, such as the Drummond or the Victoria.

Watson also applied a disguise to the hotel where the 'famous black pearl of the Borgias' was stolen from Prince Colonna's bedroom, the event that was to lead to the violent and bizarre events of 'The Six Napoleons'. The clue to the real identity of the hotel lies, as so often, in the name the doctor chose to give it, the Dacre Hotel, which tends to place it in Victoria Street. We can assume this because the Dacre estate was an extensive landowner on the north side, commemorated in Dacre Street, which survives and runs between what are now called Broadway and Dean Farrar Street, near St James's Park Underground Station. The hotel itself was almost certainly the Windsor, which Baedeker noted was 'well spoken of' and was considered important enough to be identified by name on a street map of the period. This was surely just the sort of place that would have been eminently suitable for the accommodation of Prince Colonna, who must have been of foreign royal stock. Appropriately enough in modern terms, the site of the old Windsor is just along the street from New Scotland Yard.

So far, the hotels we have visited, both under their own and assumed names, have been no more than details in Holmes's cases. The same is not true of another of Watson's genuine locations, the Charing Cross Hotel, abutting the railway station. This opened in the same year as the Langham to great admiration of the French Renaissance style of its architect, Edward Barry, who was also responsible for the Royal Opera House and the adjacent glass Floral Hall. The Charing Cross Hotel plays an important part in

Looking much as it did in its Victorian heyday, the Charing Cross Hotel is where the spy Hugo Oberstein was arrested after Holmes had solved the mystery of 'The Bruce-Partington Plans'

'The Adventure of the Bruce-Partington Plans' because it is there that Holmes traps the killer of the Woolwich Arsenal clerk.

Having caught, as we saw in the chapter on Kensington, the man who had taken the plans – the ne'er-do-well brother of a senior naval expert at the Arsenal – Holmes forces him to write to the secret agent at the heart of the case, Hugo Oberstein, claiming to have a tracing of the vital missing part of the stolen plans: 'I would come to you abroad, but it would excite remark if I left the country at present. Therefore I shall expect to meet you in the smoking-room of the Charing Cross Hotel at noon on Saturday.'

The hotel has gone through several owners and many interior redesigns and redecorations since then, 1895, and it remains a pleasant, elegant, comfortable and welcoming haven of peace in the busy Strand, though perhaps a little too marked these days by conferences, conventions and business events. The era of the smoking-room is long past, of course, and thanks to recent legislation no smoking at all is permitted inside the building. Nevertheless, one can still sit in the bar or the charming restaurant, as I have done many times over the years, and recall the day when, as Watson put it: 'It is a matter of history – that secret history of a nation which is often so much more intimate and interesting than its public chronicles – that Oberstein, eager to complete the coup of his lifetime, came to the lure and was safely engulfed for fifteen years in a British prison.'

There are other London hotels, some in disguise and at least one apparently identified correctly, that are crucial to Holmes's investigations. In 'The Noble Bachelor', for instance, it is a fragment from a hotel bill that leads him to Francis Hay Moulton, whose sudden appearance interrupted the marriage ceremony of the faithless Lord St Simon and Miss Hatty Doran the mining heiress:

Oct. 4th, rooms 8s., breakfast 2s. 6d., cocktail 1s., lunch 2s 6d., glass sherry, 8d.

Inspector Lestrade sees nothing valuable in this, preferring to concentrate on the note written on the other side of it and signed F.H.M. To Holmes, however, it is the bill as much as the note that is a vital piece of evidence leading to the solution of the mystery of the fleeing bride, as he explains to Watson after revealing to his lordship that Mr Moulton and Miss Doran are in fact man and wife.

> *'The initials were, of course, of the highest importance, but more valuable still was it to know that within a week he had settled his bill at one of the most select London hotels.'*
> *'How did you deduce the select?'*
> *'By the select prices. Eight shillings for a bed and eightpence for a glass of sherry pointed to one of the most expensive hotels. There are not many in London which charge at that rate. In the second one which I visited in Northumberland Avenue, I learned by an inspection of the book that Francis H. Moulton, an American gentleman, had left only the day before, and on looking over the entries against him, I came upon the very items which I had seen in the duplicate bill. His letters were to be forwarded to 226 Gordon Square, so thither I travelled ...'*

This is 1887, a decade or so after the compulsory purchase by the Metropolitan Board of Works of the Duke of Northumberland's London estate south of Trafalgar Square and the construction of the ambitious avenue that bears his name, which had been planned as a street of grand hotels with a theatre at the river end. At the time of Holmes's visit only two hotels had been completed in Northumberland Avenue, the Grand in 1880 and the ultra-modern and staggeringly luxurious Métropole five years later. Holmes noted that it was in the second one he visited that he had discovered the recent presence of Mr Moulton. Assuming that he had travelled from Baker Street, his first call would surely have been at the Grand, since it sat at the corner of Trafalgar Square and Northumberland Avenue, very close to Charing Cross Station. It must, therefore, surely have been at the Métropole, farther down the street, that he found the traces of his quarry.

Select it most certainly was, and deliberately so. Upon its opening, an eighty-eight-page brochure announced that the Métropole was:

The former Métropole Hotel at the Embankment end of Northumberland Avenue. It was to this luxury establishment that Holmes tracked the missing first husband of the bride in 'The Noble Bachelor'

... particularly recommended to ladies and families visiting the West End during the Season; to travellers from Paris and the Continent, arriving from Dover and Folkestone at the Charing Cross Terminus; to Officers and others attending the levees at St James; to Ladies going to the Drawing Rooms, State Balls, and Concerts at Buckingham Palace; and to colonial and American visitors unused to the great world of London.

One of the most notable features of the hotel was its semi-circular restaurant at the corner of Whitehall Place with tall French windows overlooking the Thames. There one could dine in splendour before perhaps crossing the road to the Avenue Theatre. It was at the Métropole that intrepid car drivers breakfasted before the first London to Brighton motor rally – called the Emancipation Run because it celebrated the passing of the Locomotives on

Highways Act 1896, which removed the last barriers to motoring. During the meal, the Earl of Winchelsea tore up one of the hated red flags that had previously been required to be carried in front of a car on the road. A world later, after the convulsion of the First World War, Winston Churchill was staying at the Métropole as he and the rest of the nation waited for the eleventh hour of the eleventh day of the eleventh month of 1918 for the Armistice to come into effect.

Given the grandeur of the place and the prices to match, it is hardly surprising that Francis Hay Moulton should have spent only a short amount of time there before seeking more modest lodgings in Bloomsbury.

The magnificence of the Métropole is still discernible today, though the building has fallen into a sad state. It was sold to the government in 1936 to accommodate civil servants and ultimately passed into the hands of the Ministry of Defence. By 2008, however, there were signs that the elegant building would return to its former glory, with reports that it had been bought by the International Hotel Investments group of Malta, which wished to see it rise again as a five-star hotel.

Elsewhere in Northumberland Avenue, the old Grand has been reduced to offices in a building named after it – though there is still a luxurious Grand Hotel on the opposite side of the road about halfway down, where the third great nineteenth-century shrine to exclusive hospitality, the Victoria, once stood. Also surviving is the Avenue Theatre, renamed the Playhouse.

Any of these three hotels could have been disguised as the 'Cosmopolitan', where the Countess of Morcar was staying when an employee stole her 'valuable gem known as the blue carbuncle'. They were certainly among the smartest in London at the time and some Holmes experts have suggested that the Métropole would have been the best candidate. However, Dr Watson, in his customary fashion, includes in his report of the case a tiny clue that suggests the real Hotel Cosmopolitan was elsewhere.

He quotes part of a press report in which 'Inspector Bradstreet, B division, gave evidence as to the arrest of Horner', the plumber who had had the misfortune to be in the wrong place at the wrong time and had found himself accused of the theft. A search of the archives of the Metropolitan Police reveals that when the force's seventeen original administrative areas were set up in the 1830s, B Division was based in Chelsea. In that case, what would Inspector Bradstreet have been doing making an arrest in Charing Cross? That would have been the business of a senior officer from A Division.

The date of this case is 1889 and just two years earlier the luxurious Cadogan Hotel had opened in Chelsea at number 75 Sloane Street, about halfway between Knightsbridge and Sloane Square, beside the gardens of Cadogan Place. I feel sure this was where the countess stayed, having presumably been invited to attend some grand event worthy of her precious jewel. It was certainly a favourite in London society. The Prince of Wales frequented the Cadogan – he was known to pay court to his mistress Lillie Langtry there – and another regular was Oscar Wilde, who was in fact arrested in room 118 in 1895. Today the Cadogan Hotel is still very much alive, describing itself as a place of elegantly modernized Edwardian beauty, 'a hotel with its soul rooted both in SW1 and an altogether more genteel age'.

One can see why Dr Watson would not have wanted to broadcast the real name of the hotel, since guests would have felt less than comfortable knowing that there had been a thief on the staff. He might have retained its initial letter, but identifying it on the basis of his Hotel Cosmopolitan would have required of his readers a certain knowledge of the way the London police service was organized.

Meanwhile, going back to Northumberland Avenue, we come across a real mystery involving hotels and Sherlock Holmes. It arises in *The Hound of the Baskervilles*, the only one of Holmes's cases in which Watson is present as the story unfolds inside a London hotel. In Chapter 4 of the book, the last of the Baskervilles, Sir Henry, arrives at Baker Street bringing with him a note he has received addressed to him at the 'Northumberland Hotel, Charing Cross'. This is crucial to the case, as is the subsequent theft of two of his boots at the hotel. The mystery is why Watson gave the proper name of the hotel and what on earth Sir Henry Baskerville was doing there at all.

The Northumberland Hotel of the period, proprietor William John Wright, was a relatively modest establishment at the southern end of Northumberland Street, which ran at an angle from the Strand into the newly constructed Northumberland Avenue. It occupied numbers 10 and 11 in the short street and a contemporary photograph shows it to have been a rather dismal building with large, pub-style windows on the ground floor and three storeys of rooms, including attics, above. The street in which it stood was little more prepossessing. At the top end was a livery stable and farther down were the offices of the *Pall Mall Gazette* and the *Manchester Guardian*, along with four lodging houses, three different kinds of engineering concerns and an agent for patent medicines. It does not look at all like the sort of place where the inheritor in 1889 of a stately home and a vast fortune of £740,000 would have chosen to stay on his first visit to London.

After all, just round the corner was the new Hotel Métropole, a few hundred yards away could be found the Grand, and farther along the Strand – since Sir Henry had no need to be so close to Charing Cross – there was the wonderful Savoy, another of the best hotels in town. Yet it is the little Northumberland Hotel that has gone down in history as perhaps the most visible of all the London sites related to Sherlock Holmes. It did not remain a hotel for very long, possibly because of competition from the new establishments that sprang up in the district during the 1880s and the growing demand for superior accommodation. Under new management, it became the Northumberland tavern and later the Northumberland Arms, a simple, comfortable pub. Such it remained until 1957 when its owners, the brewers Whitbread, bought an entire collection of Holmes memorabilia that had been assembled for the Festival of Britain, installed this in their pub, created a replica of the sitting room and study at 221B Baker Street and, not unnaturally, changed the name of the hostelry to The Sherlock Holmes, which it still proudly bears and which has done no harm at all to its business.

So why would Sir Henry Baskerville have ended up staying at the little Northumberland Hotel when he could easily have afforded

The Sherlock Holmes pub in Northumberland Avenue. Formerly the
Northumberland Hotel, it was the somewhat surprising choice of the newly
wealthy Sir Henry Baskerville for lodgings during his first visit to London

something considerably better, even in the same neighbourhood,
and why did Watson draw attention to his curious choice?

The answers to those two questions are related and in different ways
they both involve the matter of class. Henry Baskerville was an unexpected inheritor of his family title, a Canadian farmer ignorant of the
ways of the landed aristocracy and unused to having large sums of
money at his disposal. He had obviously managed to book his passage
to London, but he would have had no idea about where he might stay
or of how to make a choice among the bewildering number of hotels
the city offered. As he admitted when Holmes asked:

> 'Who knew that you were going to the Northumberland Hotel?'
> 'No one could have known. We only decided after I met Dr
> Mortimer.'

It was Mortimer who had travelled from Devon to bring the case of
the Baskerville 'curse' to Holmes's attention and to meet the new

In the 1880s Craven Street was rather more respectable than the neighbouring Northumberland Street, the home of surgeons, architects, surveyors, wine importers and the embassies of the republics of Uruguay and Argentina. Perhaps that is why Watson was so reticent. There were no fewer than four private hotels in the street, because of its proximity to Charing Cross Station, but my guess is that Stapleton actually stayed in the larger Craven Hotel at numbers 44 to 46, owned by Alfred Warner at the top end of the street, just off the Strand. This was not too close to Sir Henry's Northumberland Hotel but near enough to keep a discreet eye on his comings and goings. Once more the clue lies in the choice of pseudonym: Mexborough is in Yorkshire, near Doncaster; Craven is near Skipton, just a few miles farther north.

Thanks to both Watson's precision and his easily penetrated smokescreen in *The Hound of the Baskervilles*, it is possible today to come out of Charing Cross Station, or cross Trafalgar Square, or walk to the western end of the Strand, duck between the garish concrete of the shopping centres and office blocks and find ourselves in Craven Street. There, so long as we keep our eyes to the left as we walk towards the river, we can imagine ourselves back in the world of Sherlock Holmes – and end up at the pub named after him. Perhaps regrettably, Nevill's Turkish Baths are no more. They closed in 1947.

CHAPTER EIGHT

Off the Beaten Track

So far we have followed Holmes and Watson through parts of central London and also to the south, east and west of the city. These were indeed their main centres of activity, apart from Mayfair, St James's and Westminster, which we shall be visiting in the final chapter of this book. On three occasions, however – that is, three we know about – they did venture to northern parts of London to pursue what were to become some of Holmes's most exciting cases.

Of these three recorded cases, their deepest venture into northern suburbia took them to Harrow Weald, now at the very edge of the metropolitan area as part of the London borough of Harrow, but in the late nineteenth century a rural parish in the county of Middlesex, on the border of Hertfordshire. This was the setting for 'The Adventure of the Three Gables'.

The use of the word 'adventure' in the title chosen by Watson is certainly most appropriate in this case, as the doctor indicates in the opening sentence of his account: 'I don't think that any of my adventures with Mr Sherlock Holmes opened quite so abruptly, or so dramatically, as that which I associate with The Three Gables.' This was the sudden arrival at Baker Street of Steve Dixie, the boxer with gangland connections we encountered in considering Holmes's contacts in the East End, and his violent attempt to warn Holmes against acting on behalf of the elderly lady from whom he had received a plea for help, which he showed to Watson.

Dear Mr Sherlock Holmes [I read]:

I have had a succession of strange incidents occur to me in connection with this house, and I should much value your advice. You would find me at home any time to-morrow. The house is within a short walk from the Weald Station. I believe that my late husband, Mortimer Maberley, was one of your early clients ...

The address was 'The Three Gables, Harrow Weald'.

'So that's that!' said Holmes. 'And now, if you can spare the time, Watson, we will get upon our way.'

They went by train, of course, taking the London and North Western Railway's Watford service from Euston to what was officially known as Harrow and Wealdstone Station. Instead of walking from there, though, they took a short drive to meet Mrs Maberley.

The house turned out to be 'a brick and timber villa, standing in its own acre of undeveloped grassland'. Watson observed:

Three projections above the upper windows made a feeble attempt to justify its name. Behind was a grove of melancholy, half-grown pines, and the whole aspect of the place was poor and depressing. None the less, we found the house to be well furnished, and the lady who received us was a most engaging elderly person, who bore every mark of refinement and culture.

At this time, Harrow Weald had not yet experienced the real building boom that would increase its population from 1,500 or so to almost 11,000 in the space of twenty years. Mrs Maberley, evidently in straitened circumstances following the death of her husband, had settled in the best place she could afford that would offer her a retired life. She was not far enough from London, though, to protect her from the attentions of the thugs employed by the adventuress Isadora Klein, whom Mrs Maberley's dead grandson sought to expose in the manuscript of a book he had left with her.

It is impossible to locate The Three Gables in the modern suburb, with its network of residential streets leading off the High

Road, but it was probably some little distance north of the station, towards the ancient woodland that marks the highest point in Middlesex and now one of the highest in London.

That was the farthest north Holmes and Watson went in what we would now call Greater London and the latest of the three cases chronicled by Watson that involved forays in that direction. The first of them, back in 1881, found them no more than three miles north of the traditional centre of London at Charing Cross as they attempted to steal items compromising to the King of Bohemia from the home of Irene Adler in St John's Wood. The area is, of course, even closer to Baker Street, which leads into Park Road and from there takes one almost directly to St John's Wood High Street.

In view of the sensitive nature of both the case and the 'Illustrious Client', it is perfectly understandable that Watson should have gone to some trouble to cover their tracks, while doing his best to give as many details as possible of their only excursion to St John's Wood. That makes discovering where the beautiful and resourceful Miss Adler really lived something of a puzzle worthy of Holmes himself.

It was the King of Bohemia who, according to Watson, revealed her address at Holmes's request and he gives it as Briony Lodge, Serpentine Avenue. The Ordnance Survey maps of St John's Wood in the early 1880s show nothing designated as an avenue, other than Avenue Road, which skirts St John's Wood on its way from Regent's Park to Swiss Cottage. In 1881 this was actually classified as being in the district of Regent's Park but, more importantly, it contained a series of very large houses standing in extensive grounds, which does not match Watson's description of Irene Adler's home.

Perhaps, then, there is a tiny hint as to the real street in Watson's choice of the name Serpentine rather than his designation of 'Avenue'. We have already seen examples of his transliteration, but the normal connections that would have occurred to him do not seem to apply here, since no obvious street name that might have been turned into Serpentine can be found. The clue to the way his mind was working in this case might lie in the fact that the Regent's Canal snakes round the border of St John's Wood, suggesting a possible convenient cipher based on the famous lake in Hyde Park. The doctor was nothing if not observant.

At the same time, we cannot assume that Serpentine Avenue was one of the streets close to the canal. First, that area would certainly have been called Regent's Park rather than St John's Wood and, second, the kind of houses there do not match Holmes's description of Briony Lodge. It was, apparently, 'a bijou villa, with a garden at the back, but built out in front right up to the road, two stories'. That narrows down the choice. Then, when Watson visited Briony Lodge, he found it to be in 'a small street in a quiet neighbourhood' and he went on to note that Irene Adler's carriage 'came round the curve of the avenue'. So we are in a short, quiet street with a bend in it, in front of a villa with 'a mews in a lane which runs down by the wall of the garden'.

All that makes it sound as if the house should be easy enough to locate but, unfortunately for the researcher, St John's Wood is full of such properties. Developed from the beginning of the nineteenth century, it was one of the first London suburbs in which traditional terraced housing gave way in many cases to development of much lower density in the form of villas that were either in their own grounds or else semi-detached. We could be in Carlton Hill, or Blenheim Road, or the upper part of Hamilton Terrace or a variety of other streets. All of those contain the sort of villas that might match Irene Adler's.

One difficulty, however, is that the layout of the streets meant that a mews behind the houses was found far less than in the terraced streets such as Abbey Gardens. I did find on a contemporary map one detached villa with a mews approached by a lane along the side of the garden, in Clifton Hill, but that could not have been where Irene Adler lived because it is shown to have a large front garden separating it from the road and its size indicated that it would never have been described by Holmes as bijou.

An additional constraint in locating the real house is that Watson speaks of Miss Adler's carriage coming round the curve of the avenue as he and Holmes keep watch outside. Because the development of St John's Wood was carefully planned, most of the streets are quite straight, with barely a curve anywhere. Grove End Road is an exception, so could this have been where Irene Adler lived?

As a noted opera singer she would have been in congenial company. The street was full of artists, no fewer than nine of them, including the popular painter of landscapes George Herbig and the French portraitist and caricaturist Jacques Tissot, who lived there with his model and mistress Kathleen Newton. Indeed there were so many painters, sculptors and engravers in the neighbourhood that one group of them was known in the art world as 'The St John's Wood Clique' and in 1880 the St John's Wood Art School had been founded in Elm Tree Road, behind Lord's Cricket Ground, to prepare students for entry to the Royal Academy Schools. Yet we are still wide of the mark here. Not only was Grove End Road a broad thoroughfare rather than a short, quiet street, but it was also lined with very large properties such as Grove House and Weston Lodge, protected by their own grounds and often approached by sweeping carriage drives. There were about a dozen villas at the northern end of the road, but again they are different in character from the one we are seeking.

The same is true of Circus Road, which leads off Grove End and also features a gentle curve. The villas here were much more substantial and on larger plots than the one identified by Holmes and Watson.

'I soon found Briony Lodge,' Holmes told Watson after reconnoitring the house disguised as 'a drunken-looking groom, ill-kempt and side-whiskered, with an inflamed face and disreputable clothes'. He must have had more luck than I did as I tramped the delightful, tree-lined streets of St John's Wood on a rather too-warm spring day, gazing at the rows of pretty villas that still distinguish this exclusive and cosmopolitan area.

It was only after lunch outdoors in the attractive High Street that I turned a corner into St John's Wood Terrace and found myself in front of a two-storey villa with, as Holmes described it, 'a large sitting-room on the right side ... with long windows almost to the floor'. The resemblance was not exact. For one thing, this

in which Milverton lived, but Watson is very circumspect in describing the large house to which he gave the fictional name of Appledore Towers. We are not even told the name of the road in which it was situated, so that finding it would be well-nigh impossible. Hampstead has been characterized as 'a huge collection of twists and turns … a large collection of roads and passages which don't go in straight lines'. All we do know is that Holmes and Watson, having taken a cab to Church Row in Hampstead, walked 'along the edge of the heath' to reach Milverton's house, which Holmes intended to burgle on behalf of his distraught client, Lady Eva Blackwell.

Church Row is a narrowish lane leading off the southern end of Heath Street, at the back of Hampstead High Street. No doubt it was a convenient spot at which a cab from Baker Street could drop them, since it would have gone straight up Park Road to Finchley Road, through Swiss Cottage and along Fitzjohn's Avenue. According to Holmes, Church Row was 'a quarter of an hour's walk' from Appledore Towers, but it leads away from rather than towards the heath, so which way did they go in order to reach Milverton's house by the route Watson suggested?

Crossing Heath Road and Rosslyn Hill, then cutting through Flask Walk, they could have reached the heath by going down Well Walk but, although there are large houses in the area, they tend to be fairly close together among a network of roads, and we are given the impression that Appledore Towers was rather more isolated. In any case, it would not have taken them a quarter of an hour to reach that part of Hampstead from Church Row. My guess is that they struck north up Heath Street towards what are known as the Vale of Health and North End. That way they would have come to West Heath, which they then skirted to bring them close to a number of large houses, among them Ash Mount, The Turrets, Spedan Tower and The Glade. The area looks very much like Appledore Towers territory. The properties were private and secure in their own grounds but near enough to others – in Branch Hill, for example, or Redington Road – for the alarm to have been raised quickly at the sound of the fatal shots fired at Milverton by one of his previous victims. As Watson recalled:

One fellow raised a view-halloa as we emerged from the veranda and
followed hard at our heels. Holmes seemed to know the grounds
perfectly, and he threaded his way among a plantation of small trees
… It was a six-foot wall that barred our path, but he sprang to the top
and over … I fell upon my face among some small bushes, but
Holmes had me on my feet in an instant, and together we dashed
away across the huge expanse of Hampstead Heath. We had run two
miles, I suppose, before Holmes halted …

Since those days there has been a good deal of building in the area,
names have changed and new roads have appeared. Some of the old
places are still there, however, and it must be that in one of them,
behind high walls, the murder of Charles Augustus Milverton, 'one
of the most dangerous men in London', was committed before the
very eyes of Sherlock Holmes and Dr Watson.

So end our visits to north London, but not Holmes's expeditions
beyond what we might call today his 'comfort zone'. When we
followed him south of the Thames, we found ourselves briefly as far
away as Upper Norwood, but for the most part we spent our time
in places closer to home such as Brixton, Camberwell and
Kennington. There were other cases, though, that took the
intrepid pursuers farther out into the developing suburbs of the
capital. Among them was Streatham, south of Brixton, a village
originally joined to London by the Brighton turnpike and noted
mainly for its health-giving springs until rich City merchants
began to colonize it from the middle of the eighteenth century.
The arrival of the railways increased its popularity and tempted to
Streatham people like Alexander Holder, the senior banker
embroiled in the affair of 'The Beryl Coronet' in 1886.

Mr Holder was the very model of the wealthy, solid, suburban
respectability that marked the Streatham of the period: 'He was a
man of about fifty, tall, portly, and imposing, with a massive,
strongly marked face and a commanding figure. He was dressed in
a sombre yet rich style, in black frock-coat, shining hat, neat
brown gaiters, and well-cut pearl-grey trousers.' Not for him,
either, the delusions of grandeur that had prompted the brewer
Ralph Thrale to construct a Georgian mansion at Streatham Park,

on land he had bought from the Duke of Bedford. The banker's house, Fairbank – a good suburban name, that, with its rural connotations – was characterized by Watson as 'modest'. He seemed faintly surprised that it should be the residence of a great financier:

> *Fairbank was a good-sized square house of white stone, standing back a little from the road. A double carriage-sweep, with a snow-clad lawn, stretched down in front of two large iron gates which closed the entrance. On the right side was a small wooden thicket, which led into a narrow path between two neat hedges stretching from the road to the kitchen door, and forming the tradesmen's entrance. On the left ran a lane which led to the stables, and was not itself within the grounds at all, being a public, though little used, thoroughfare ...*

There are still a few substantial properties 'a short walk', as Watson put it, from the railway station, but most have disappeared under the successive waves of speculative building that produced the serried ranks of terraces and semi-detached villas in the area, an area which also provided the location for the forerunner of the Sainsbury's supermarket chain at the end of the nineteenth century. In fact, between the two world wars, Streatham was perhaps best known as a centre for shopping and entertainment, with what was classed as the 'busiest high street' in south London on the one hand and the Ice Rink, Locarno Ballroom and Streatham Hill Theatre on the other. After the Second World War, however, there began a long period of decline and abandonment by better-off residents. As recently as 2002 Streatham High Road came top of a poll designed to identify 'the worst street in Britain'.

Perhaps stung by its unwelcome award, Streatham began to pull itself together and today its tree-lined streets, its Common, the revitalized Streatham Green and the beginning of refurbishment in the High Road, attract middle-class families who rub shoulders with large numbers of asylum seekers from Africa. Described recently as a 'hip' south London neighbourhood, it is a very long way from the world of Alexander Holder.

Perhaps rather less changed in character, allowing for modern developments and a greater and more diverse population, is Lewisham, home of 'The Retired Colourman', Josiah Amberley, whom we met earlier on Dr Watson's uncomfortable train journey to Essex. Even then, Watson was writing of 'the monotonous brick streets, the weary suburban highways', among which Mr Amberley's The Haven was 'a little island of ancient culture and comfort', an old home 'surrounded by a high sun-baked wall and topped with moss'. This was 1898, about the time when the writer E. Nesbit, most famous for *The Railway Children* and a one-time resident of both Lewisham and nearby Eltham, wrote that, 'In London, or at any rate Lewisham, nothing happens unless you make it happen; or if it happens it doesn't happen to you, and you don't know the people it does happen to.'

Against that background, the double murder committed by Josiah Amberley was obviously a sensation, 'The Haven Horror' as it was headlined above extensive coverage in the local newspaper. The house was apparently 'only a few hundred yards' from the police station, but we do not know in which direction. Watson's comment about the weary suburban highways might suggest it was close to Lewisham High Street, off which were several terraces that hid older detached properties. The police station at the time was in Ladywell, in the southern part of the town, where one of a dozen or so of the only surviving ancient roads in Lewisham was to be found, with some properties to match it amid the new buildings that had gone up around the end of the nineteenth century. Many of the older, larger houses had already been demolished by developers in the 1890s and one can only assume that The Haven soon followed them, not least because of the evil reputation it acquired as a result of Holmes's investigation. The police station, too, is no longer there, replaced in 2004 by one that has been officially declared the largest in Europe, between Lee High Road and Myron Place, at the northern end of the High Street.

A decade earlier than his encounter with Josiah Amberley, Holmes had travelled well south of Lewisham and Streatham for 'The Adventure of the Cardboard Box', in which the straitlaced Miss Susan Cushing received through the post two severed ears – not a pair, as Holmes quickly pointed out:

'One of these ears is a woman's, small, finely formed and pierced for an earring. The other is a man's, sunburned, discoloured, and also pierced for an earring. These two people are presumably dead, or we should have heard their story before now ... If the two people were murdered, who but their murderer would have sent this sign of his work to Miss Cushing?'

The lady lived in Cross Street, Croydon, a place first settled by the Saxons in the eighth century and subsequently the largest town in Surrey until it became a London borough in 1965. It is the town's modern status that justifies its inclusion in this Holmesian travelogue, but even in the 1880s it qualified as something of a suburb of the capital, having been served in 1803 by the first public railway in the world, with trains drawn by horses, and half a century later by the London to Brighton line.

Cross Street, Watson tells us, was five minutes' walk from the station and 'it was a very long street of two-storey brick houses, neat and prim, with whitened stone steps and little groups of aproned women gossiping at the doors'. He does not reveal at which Croydon station – West, the older one, or East – they arrived, but my researches indicate that it must have been East Croydon. There is no Cross Street in the district but there was a Cross Road, which is about a five-minute walk away from the station. Moreover, when Holmes and Watson left Miss Cushing's house they were able to hail a passing cab, which suggests they were near main roads, and Cross Road is between two of them, running between Lower Addiscombe Road, now part of the A222, and Cherry Orchard Road. It is also a long street of two-storey houses, though greatly changed in appearance since the women in white aprons stood gossiping on their doorsteps.

Watson comments that on his visit the heat in Croydon was much less oppressive than in London, but the lighter air did not make it any healthier at the time. In fact, so bad had public health been that the town had formed the first Local Health Board in Britain, and the year after Holmes had there solved the case of the severed ears the authorities embarked upon a vast scheme of slum clearance which was to continue for half a century. There was no stopping the migration of the middle classes to the leafier, more open parts of the town, however, and the Croydon that has resulted would have been a revelation to Holmes and Watson with its tall office blocks, cultural centres and extensive shopping malls. They might perhaps appreciate the trams, which made their reappearance in Croydon in 2000 and are part of an infrastructure that makes it an important satellite town rather than a suburb.

One visit to Croydon was sufficient for Holmes to draw together all the elements of the murder of Miss Cushing's sister and her lover, but another suburban case, that of 'The Norwood Builder', called for more extensive journeyings through the outer reaches of south-east London. Although it was in Lower Norwood that the supposed murder of the builder Jonas Oldacre by his young legatee Hector McFarlane had taken place, it was to Blackheath that Holmes first travelled to interview the parents of the suspect. Here we are probably not among the grand Georgian houses in this historic and still sought-after area in which the SE3 postcode adds a premium to the price of a house compared with the neighbouring SE7, but perhaps on the western side, closer to Greenwich. There, in places like Westcombe Park Road, Mycenae Road and Charlton Road, were villas with names such as Ivydene, New Forest Lodge, Meadow Bank and Marlborough Lodge and they seem to fit with the Torrington Lodge that McFarlane had given Holmes as his address.

Finding nothing to help him in Blackheath, as he told Watson, Holmes went off to Norwood. He must have taken the train to London Bridge and changed there for West Norwood. 'Deep Dene House', he reported when he returned to Baker Street, 'is a big modern villa of staring brick, standing back in its own grounds, with a laurel-clumped lawn in front of it. To the right and some distance back was the timber yard', which had been the scene of the fire in which Jonas Oldacre's body had apparently been burned. From an account of the affair in *The Daily Telegraph* quoted by Watson we further learn that the house was at the Sydenham end of the road of that name. This is confusing. Sydenham Road would place us in Lower Sydenham rather than Lower Norwood, in which case Holmes would have taken the train to Sydenham Station. Equally, if that was the true location of Deep Dene House,

and Croydon mayor jailed in 1893 for his part in the Liberator Building Society fraud, which brought financial ruin to thousands of ordinary savers and is said to have been responsible for a number of suicides. The hall is now an old people's home.

The description given to Sherlock Holmes by Mr Munro suggests that he and his wife lived south and west of the Norbury Station of the Croydon and Balham Railway, which had been operating since 1862, although the station itself did not appear until 1878. According to a contemporary map, the main road linking Norbury with Croydon was dotted with houses, but a mile or so along it, just before Thornton House and on the Thornton Heath side of the main road, was a narrow lane leading to a small enclave which did indeed include an inn and also contained a wooded area that could well have been the one characterized by Mr Munro as 'a nice little grove of Scotch firs'. It was here, at the cottage across the field, that he had seen the yellow face at the window and where he subsequently found his wife.

Further evidence of the location comes from Mr Munro when he tells Holmes that, after confronting his wife about her connection with the cottage and the yellow face and receiving no explanation, he had left his house and walked to Crystal Palace, where he had spent an hour in the grounds. He would have gone directly from his home via Thornton Heath to Upper Norwood and from there up Church Road to the palace, a relatively easy walk.

After hearing the story, Holmes told Mr Munro to return to Norbury and wire him if he discovered any further activity at the cottage. When a wire was received, Holmes and Watson dashed to Victoria Station and took the seven o'clock train. Met by Mr Munro, they set off in the rain to walk down the tree-lined lane to the cottage, where they were met by Mrs Munro and discovered that Holmes's theoretical solution to the mystery was completely wrong. He had assumed that Mrs Munro's former husband, supposedly dead in America, had returned to blackmail her and had set himself up in the cottage in order to do so. In fact, it was a daughter that she had been hiding and disguising with a mask – the child of 'a man strikingly handsome and intelligent-looking, but bearing unmistakable signs upon his features of his African descent'.

It was, as Watson noted in his preface to the account, one of those rare occasions when Holmes's deductive brilliance had shown itself to be fallible, though in this case 'even when he erred the truth was discovered'. That surely earns Norbury an honoured place in the Sherlock Holmes canon.

CHAPTER NINE

Fashionable Quarters

Baker Street as it was configured in the late nineteenth century was far from being the best address in London, or even in the West End, but it was certainly within easy reach of some of the best addresses. This became evident fairly early in the association of Holmes and Watson when they received an unexpected visit from Dr Percy Trevelyan, who expressed concern about the increasingly bizarre behaviour of the wealthy patient in whose house he had been set up in practice. Wrote Watson:

> As our visitor concluded, Holmes sprang up without a word, handed me my hat, picked his own from the table, and followed Dr Trevelyan to the door. Within a quarter of an hour we had been dropped at the door of the physician's residence in Brook Street.

The doctor had arrived in a brougham and it was in that they were transported to Brook Street, although they could easily have walked from Baker Street in a quarter of an hour or less. All they had to do was take Orchard Street to Oxford Street, cross the road and walk down North Audley Street to Grosvenor Square and turn left. Watson gives the number in the street as 309, which he invented of course. The highest number at the time was 88. However, we might assume that Dr Trevelyan's house was towards the Hanover Square end, probably somewhere near South Molton Street, for Watson described it as 'one of those sombre, flat-faced houses which one associates with a West End practice'.

It was, incidentally, in Hanover Square, at St George's Church, that the supposed marriage of Lord St Simon and Miss Hatty Doran took place and led to the investigation of the mystery of 'The Noble Bachelor'. As it still is today, the elegant, early eighteenth-century church, with its impressive colonnaded entrance, was a most desirable venue for high society and fashionable weddings. That being so, the intrusion of a woman who alleged that 'she had some claim upon Lord St Simon' and the subsequent flight of the 'bride' was bound to cause quite a sensation in the popular press.

The part of Brook Street closer to Hanover Square than Grosvenor Square was at the time where most of the doctors were grouped: two of them at number 38, Henry de Meric at 52, Richard Sandon Gutteridge and David Wilson at 58 and 62 respectively and, on the south side of the street, beyond Claridge's, John Harley, James Palfrey and Robert Farquharson. From Davies Street to Grosvenor Square the houses were rather grander, occupied by such as the Earl of Dunmore, the Dowager Duchess of Cleveland and Viscount Powerscourt.

Even the doctors in that western part of the street were of the superior sort. One was William Scovell Savory, who at the time was about to become surgeon-extraordinary to Queen Victoria and would subsequently be made a baronet. Close by lived Sir William Jenner, physician to the Queen and the Prince of Wales. He was best known for his work at the London Fever Hospital, where he had discovered the difference between typhoid and typhus. His neighbour was Sir William Gull, born the son of a barge-keeper but who rose to become one of the leading clinicians of his day. He would later gain notoriety by being identified as a suspect in the Jack the Ripper murders by supporters of the conspiracy theory involving the royal family and the Freemasons. Given the proximity of such exalted company, Dr Trevelyan must have made a tidy income courtesy of the former bank robber Blessington.

From Grosvenor Square it is but a short walk down to Berkeley Square, where Holmes found himself for one of his later cases, 'The

Adventure of the Illustrious Client', at the turn of the century. It was an address as exclusive as it is now, the parental home of Miss Violet de Merville, 'rich, beautiful, accomplished, a wonder-woman in every way', who had fallen under the spell of the dangerous adventurer Baron Gruner. The house was, observed Holmes, 'one of those awful grey London castles which would make a church look frivolous'. That would not have accorded with the view of the residents of this select enclave, either then or now. Developed in the middle of the eighteenth century, Berkeley Square attracted an elevated class of inhabitant, including Clive of India, who committed suicide at number 45 in 1774.

Among the neighbours of the De Merville family in the early 1900s were the Earl of Rosebery, the Marquess of Lansdowne, Lord Annaly and Lady Dorchester, the Countess of Selkirk and a certain Sir Alfred Harmsworth, future Lord Northcliffe, founder of the *Daily Mail* and, at about this time, financial rescuer of *The Times* and *The Observer*. Today the square is still mostly residential, though frequently clogged by traffic and containing some commercial properties, and as exclusive as it ever was.

It was in the midst of this case that Holmes suffered a vicious attack in the West End, to which I referred earlier, when stick-wielding thugs working for Baron Gruner set upon him outside the Café Royal in Regent Street. The injured detective was rushed down Haymarket and through Trafalgar Square to the Charing Cross Hospital, which had grown to occupy a large site in Agar Street, off the Strand. The famous old building can still be seen today, though now taken up by a police station, the hospital having been moved out to Fulham Palace Road in 1973.

After treatment, Holmes was permitted to return to Baker Street and began to form a plan to prevent the planned marriage of Miss de Merville and Baron Gruner. As part of this, Watson was sent to the London Library to gather as much knowledge as he could about Chinese ceramics in order to gain access to Gruner, who was an authority on the subject. At the north-west corner of St James's Square, off Pall Mall, the library had not long before been rebuilt as one of the first steel-framed constructions in the capital. It has since been much extended and remains one of

London's most valuable cultural resources. For an annual member-ship of £375 or a temporary reference fee of £10 a day, users have access to more than a million books on some fifteen miles of shelves.

In St James's Square, Watson was very much in the territory of Mycroft Holmes, Sherlock's elder brother, whom we first met in the case of 'The Greek Interpreter' back in 1888. 'Mycroft has his rails and he runs on them,' said Holmes. 'His Pall Mall lodgings, the Diogenes Club, Whitehall – that is his cycle.' In view of Mycroft's sensitive position in the government as a sort of senior intelligence officer, working with the Foreign Office in Whitehall and the War Office in Pall Mall, Watson is naturally reluctant to give any detailed information about his 'rails'.

He does quote Holmes as saying that his brother 'walks round the corner into Whitehall every morning and back every evening', which suggests that his lodgings might have been towards the eastern end of Pall Mall. One cannot in fact simply walk round the corner from there into Whitehall, though this might just have been Holmes's shorthand for a route that would have followed Cockspur Street, the south side of Trafalgar Square and Charing Cross into Whitehall. However, Mycroft could not have lodged in the section of Pall Mall between Waterloo Place and Cockspur Street because the Royal Opera Arcade was on one side of the street and there were only commercial properties on the other.

If Mycroft lived in the blocks west of Waterloo Place he could still have in effect walked round the corner by taking the Duke of York steps in the middle of Carlton House Terrace down to Horse Guards and across the edge of St James's Park.

Had he been on the north side, he might have had rooms in Jacob Ratcliffe's lodging house near the corner of John Street, or else in the house at number 26, which contained several gentlemen's apartments. There were also multiple occupants in the next block, forming the south side of St James's Square, and they were mostly military men, no doubt working at the War Office, which was facing them. On the southern side of Pall Mall, Mycroft could have been one of the residents of Reform Chambers, which were home to a number of members of parliament, but this is unlikely because Holmes tells us that his lodgings were 'just opposite' his club and most of the clubs for which Pall Mall had become famous were on the south side.

To help us come closer to the exact locations of both the lodgings and the so-called Diogenes Club, we must follow Holmes and Watson on one of their walks. Summoned by Mycroft to hear the disturbing story of Mr Melas, 'the chief Greek interpreter in London', they leave Baker Street and walk along Oxford Street towards Regent Circus. They cannot have gone too far in that direction, though, because Watson tells us that 'We had reached Pall Mall as we talked and were walking down it from the St James's Street end'.

St James's Street is on the south side of Piccadilly opposite Albemarle Street, but the latter does not reach back to Oxford Street, so my guess is that their walk took them down Davies Street into Berkeley Square and then to Berkeley Street and on to Piccadilly, where they would have turned right where the Ritz Hotel now stands. Since the hotel did not open until 1906, what Holmes and Watson would have seen on its site would have been a stationer's shop, a dealer in stable fittings, a brush maker, an advertising agency, a newsagent and a solicitor's office. In St James's Street they would have passed several bookshops, tailors and hatters, wine merchants and gentlemen's clubs, including White's, Boodle's and Brooks's, all three of which are still very much alive. Turning into Pall Mall, the two of them continued a little way until:

> Sherlock Holmes stopped at a door some little distance from the Carlton, and, cautioning me not to speak, he led the way into the hall. Through the glass panelling I caught a glimpse of a large and luxurious room, in which a considerable number of men were sitting about reading papers, each in his own little nook.

This was the Diogenes Club, described by Holmes as the queerest club in London.

> 'There are many men in London, you know, who, some from shyness, some from misanthropy, have no wish for the company of

their fellows. Yet they are not averse to comfortable chairs and the latest periodicals. It is for the convenience of these that the Diogenes Club was started, and it now contains the most unsociable and unclubbable men in town. No member is permitted to take the least notice of any other one. Save in the Stranger's Room, no talking is, under any circumstances, allowed, and three offences, if brought to the notice of the committee, render the talker liable to expulsion. My brother was one of the founders, and I have myself found it a very soothing atmosphere.'

For the reason that I indicated earlier, the Diogenes Club was obviously not the real name of the place, and much effort has been expended over the years in trying to penetrate the disguise. Many have suggested the Athenaeum, at 107 Pall Mall, on the corner of Waterloo Place, but that cannot be correct. Although it might be said to be at some little distance from the Carlton Club, being at the end of the block on the east side of Carlton Gardens, the Athenaeum was founded essentially for public figures in the arts, science and literature and would have therefore been unlikely to ban talking. Most tellingly, the dates are wrong. If Mycroft was Sherlock's senior by seven years, which we are told he was, then he could not have been one of the founders of the Athenaeum because he would not have been born in 1824.

Nor was the Carlton Club itself, then at 94 Pall Mall, the model for the Diogenes. Apart from the fact that it was founded only six years after the Athenaeum, its principal role was political, in the interest of the Tory party, for which it had served as headquarters until 1860. Indeed, in 'The Adventure of the Illustrious Client', it was from the Carlton Club that Holmes received a message sent by the society 'fixer' Colonel Sir James Damery, who wished to seek his intervention in Miss de Merville's unfortunate love affair. The Carlton moved out of Pall Mall after the building was bombed during the Second World War and is now in St James's Street.

Similarly, the Reform Club, which once faced the Carlton and today continues to flourish at 104 Pall Mall, can be ruled out. It, too, was a political establishment, founded by members of the Whig party and subsequently a centre of Liberalism. One of the first of the London clubs to offer overnight accommodation to members, the Reform is now very much associated with civil servants, many of them from the Treasury, though its purposes are social rather than political.

Next door, at number 106, is the Travellers' Club, the oldest such establishment in Pall Mall, to where it moved from Waterloo Place in 1821. Again, this cannot have been the real location of the Diogenes, having been founded, as its name suggests, for gentlemen who had spent time abroad and wished to entertain foreign dignitaries, and having significantly predated Mycroft Holmes's birth.

What we have to look for, then, is one of the smaller clubs in Pall Mall, which have perhaps not survived in the way their more illustrious neighbours have done. We need not consider the Oxford and Cambridge University Club, which is still in existence, or the Guards Club, now the Cavalry and Guards and transplanted to the Hyde Park end of Piccadilly. The Wanderers' Club, mentioned by Charles Dickens Junior in his *Dictionary of London* as being 'for members of town and country society, and for gentlemen who have associated in various parts of the world', does not look like a potential candidate either. Mycroft Holmes was certainly not a traveller, if we are to believe the account of his brother, and he did not move in society, either town or country.

The Marlborough Club, 'a convenient and agreeable place of meeting for a Society of Gentlemen' and with limited restrictions on smoking, could be a possibility, but it was on the wrong side of the road and its foundation in 1868 at the instigation of the Prince of Wales would still be a little early for Mycroft Holmes, who would have been only nineteen or twenty years old at the time. The old Beaconsfield Club was on the south side of Pall Mall, but at what would seem to be the wrong end of the street if Watson's brief description of the location is to be trusted.

It begins to look as if the Diogenes Club – the name refers to the notoriously anti-social behaviour of the eponymous ancient-Greek philosopher – might not have been in Pall Mall itself, but else-where in St James's, and that Watson altered its location for reasons of secrecy. One possibility might have been the Windham

Club in St James's Square, which would have been round the corner from Mycroft's rooms, but once again we find that he was too young to have been among the founders. Another potential candidate could be the Orleans Club nearby, which subsequently merged with the Windham. Alternatively, we could accept that the Diogenes did not actually advertise itself as a club, owing to the fact that its members were fundamentally unclubbable, and occupied a building that looked like a private residence, of which there were a few in Pall Mall.

It has even been suggested that the Diogenes was not really a club at all, but a meeting place for members of what constituted the British Secret Service, in which case it would probably not have been far from the War Office, or perhaps actually part of it. That would explain both the ban on talking and the involvement of Mycroft Holmes, who, according to his brother, had 'a small office under the British government' and 'occasionally he is the British government'.

Holmes was in club land again to gain information about the adventuress Isadora Klein from the gossip writer Langdale Pike in the case of 'The Three Gables'. Watson observed: 'Langdale Pike was his human book of reference upon all matters of social scandal. This strange, languid creature spent his waking hours in the bow window of a St James's Street club.'

This must have been the venerable White's, the oldest gentlemen's club in London, which is famous for its window, added to the façade at 37–38 St James's Street during the Regency period and where Beau Brummel once held court. It was at this window that one of the great bets of history took place, when the Prince Regent's friend Lord Alvanley wagered £3,000 on which of two raindrops would be first to arrive at the bottom of a pane. The bet had to be called off because the two drops joined together on their way down.

Langdale Pike must have been well connected, perhaps one of the younger sons of a great aristocratic family whose fortune would have passed him by. Membership of White's was restricted and by election, although it was once said that anyone who 'ties a good knot in his handkerchief, keeps his hands out of his breeches pockets, and says nothing' could become a member – always provided, of course, that he came from an acceptable social background. The fact that Langdale Pike had not only been elected to membership but was also able to spend his time seated by the bow window speaks for itself. In his day, fellow members of White's included the Prince of Wales (later King Edward VII), Prince Arthur, Duke of Connaught, the Dukes of Devonshire and Portland, the Marquess of Lansdowne, the Earl of Dartmouth and Baron Rothschild.

'He made, it was said, a four-figure income,' wrote Dr Watson, 'by the paragraphs which he contributed every week to the garbage papers which cater to an inquisitive public. If ever, far down in the turbid depths of London life there was some strange swirl or eddy, it was marked with automatic exactness by this human dial upon the surface.'

Then as now, celebrity gossip was the stock-in-trade of the popular press, except that in those days it was often members of the aristocracy and other higher echelons of society, rather than film stars, pop idols and television personalities, whose indiscretions provided the copy, so that the most successful gossip writers would have had to have access to the best circles. Watson certainly placed this particular purveyor of social scandal in deep disguise, having replaced his real name with that of a well-known Cumbrian wilderness.

Leaving St James's and following the route Mycroft Holmes took to work, we can continue down Whitehall and find ourselves at Downing Street and the Foreign Office, the scene of the theft of 'The Naval Treaty'. Or was it? From details given in the story, we might suspect that it was actually in the Colonial Office, on the corner of Whitehall and Downing Street, that Watson's old school friend Percy Phelps found the vital treaty missing from his office. Phelps tells Watson that he had risen to a responsible position 'through the influence of my uncle, Lord Holdhurst', who had 'become foreign minister in this administration'. The government in question was Disraeli's second, in which the foreign secretary was Lord Salisbury and the under-secretary of state Sir James Fergusson. There is no obvious link to the name Holdhurst there. However, the under-secretary of state in the Colonial Office, next door to the Foreign Office, was the Earl of Onslow: his country seat was in Surrey and Holdhurst is the name of a district in the same county, which might easily have provided a cipher for Watson.

Of course it is possible that Phelps had been found a position in the Foreign Office thanks to his uncle and it was simply on the recommendation of the under-secretary of state for the colonies that he had been selected as the most trustworthy man to copy the treaty, which would have been the business of the foreign secretary rather than the Colonial Office. Yet there is a further problem. It is suggested that the thief gained entry to his office from a side-door in Charles Street, but there was no such door leading to the Foreign Office. In order to reach it, an interloper would have had to pass under an archway from Charles Street and cross the large courtyard. Perhaps, then, it was really the India Office, which did have an entrance on Charles Street, where Phelps worked.

These days the Foreign Office occupies the entire building that once also housed the Colonial Office, the India Office and, for a time, the Home Office. Curiously, the entrance to the main building is in what is now called King Charles Street.

The Foreign Office features in another case from the same year, 1887, 'The Adventure of the Second Stain'. This involves the disappearance of another critical document, this time 'a letter from a foreign potentate' which could 'lead to European complications … peace or war may hang upon the issue'. The theft actually takes place at the home of a fictional 'Secretary for European Affairs' – presumably a Foreign Office minister – in what Dr Watson calls Whitehall Terrace. By this he must mean Whitehall Gardens, a few yards north of Downing Street, which in those days contained private houses including those of some senior politicians and civil servants.

Stolen by Trelawney Hope's blackmailed wife, the letter makes its way to the home of the foreign agent Eduardo Lucas in Godolphin Street, Westminster, 'one of the old-fashioned and secluded rows of eighteenth-century houses which lie between the river and the Abbey, almost in the shadow of the great Tower of the Houses of Parliament'. The street name must be pure invention on Watson's part. Godolphin has strong West Country associations, but I can find nothing of that sort among the names of the streets leading off what is now Millbank. Perhaps we might speculate that Godolphin was the doctor's code for Lord North Street, substituting the name of a seventeenth-century political leader for that of one who flourished in the eighteenth century. In 1887 it was known simply as North Street. At all events, there are still enough eighteenth-century houses – 'narrow-chested, prim, formal and solid' – in the neighbourhood to recall the one in which Holmes was able to deduce where the missing document had been hidden by matching the bloodstain on the carpet to that on the floor beneath it.

Much easier to identify is the Westminster home of the Lord St Simon who figures in 'The Noble Bachelor'. Watson tells us that his lordship lived in Grosvenor Mansions, and that the mansions were in Victoria Street, between James Street and Spencer Street

Lord North Street, Westminster, still contains the 'narrow-chested, prim, formal and solid' houses which Watson identified as Godolphin Street, the home of the secret agent Eduardo Lucas, murdered in the case of 'The Second Stain'

on the site of what is now Westminster City Hall. In that case, of course, Holmes did not find it necessary to visit his client's home, nor that of the father of the runaway bride in Lancaster Gate, a short walk from Baker Street on the other side of Marble Arch. He and Holmes *were* in the Marble Arch area, though, to investigate the strange affair of 'The Three Garridebs' in 1902.

This involved the attempt by the notorious American criminal Killer Evans to lure Mr Nathan Garrideb out of his home in order to get his hands on a machine left in the basement by 'the greatest counterfeiter London ever saw'. For this we are in Little Ryder Street, 'one of the smaller offshoots from the Edgware Road, within a stone-cast of old Tyburn Tree', where Mr Garrideb lives on the ground floor of an 'old-fashioned Georgian edifice, with a flat brick face broken only by two deep bay windows'.

The hanging tree of Tyburn was west of the site of Marble Arch by the corner of Edgware Road and, two streets back from it, we find the short western part of Seymour Street, which runs up to Connaught Square. There, at number 72, was a house owned by Richard Nash which was divided into apartments. 'The house', according to Watson, 'had a common stair, and there were a number of names painted in the hall, some indicating offices and some private chambers. It was not a collection of residential flats, but rather the abode of Bohemian bachelors.'

Seymour Street is the shortest offshoot from Edgware Road with the exception of Connaught Place, where there were no apartments at the time. It must have been Seymour Street where Watson, in the course of arresting Killer Evans, received a gunshot wound in the thigh and saw for the only time in his long association with Holmes 'a glimpse of a great heart as well as a great brain'.

They would have walked from Baker Street to what Watson called Little Ryder Street, since the longer southern section of Seymour Street runs from Edgware Road to Portman Square, a few doors from their apartment. We have plenty of evidence that they also walked in the other direction, to what is now Oxford Circus and on down Regent Street, where some of their favourite shops were located.

In the days of Holmes and Watson, Oxford Street was already acquiring the reputation that would lead to its becoming the busiest and most crowded shopping street in Europe. It had first been developed in the eighteenth century as a place of entertainment, both indoor and outdoor, and featured on the site where Marks & Spencer now stands at number 173, east of Oxford Circus, the classically inspired assembly rooms and theatre known as the Pantheon. Opened in 1772, the Pantheon contained under its central, Turkish-inspired rotunda, one of the largest rooms in the country. On its opening night, 1,700 people paid the then astronomical sum of £50 to rub shoulders with dukes, duchesses and various other ranks of the nobility. Not only was the price prohibitive but admission also depended on the endorsement of a peeress, though commercial considerations soon led to the removal of that requirement.

By the middle of the nineteenth century the popularity of the Pantheon had run its course. The building was rebuilt first as a bazaar and later converted again into the offices and showrooms of the wine merchants and distillers W. and A. Gilbey, a name that continues to be associated with alcohol. It was demolished in 1937, when Marks & Spencer acquired the site.

The rest of the street, too, had changed considerably by the time it was frequented by Holmes and Watson. Originally a Roman road and one of the main routes out of London, it later went under several names – Tyburn Road, Oxford Road, Uxbridge Road, Worcester Road – until its present nomenclature was adopted in the early eighteenth century. Fittingly, it was the Earl of Oxford, who had become a large landowner in the area, who was largely responsible for the development of the street, which rapidly moved from being a centre of various kinds of entertainment to being a hub of commerce, especially retailing.

In the nineteenth century, the western part of it became popularly known as Ladies' Mile on account of the numbers of dressmakers and outfitters, drapers, perfumers, milliners and jewellers to be found there. Among them was a silk mercer's named John Lewis, on the corner of Holles Street, which would, of course, grow to become one of the country's great department store groups, its flagship remaining firmly where it all began in Oxford Street. John Lewis was subsequently joined by: Selfridge's, which opened in 1909; Debenhams, originally known as Marshall and Snelgrove, which moved from its original home in Wigmore Street; and D.H. Evans, now House of Fraser. Today there are more than three hundred shops in Oxford Street.

At the western end of the street, where it meets Hyde Park at Speakers' Corner, is one of London's best-known landmarks, Marble Arch. Built of Carrara marble in 1828 to John Nash's design on the model of a triumphal arch in ancient Rome, it stood originally in The Mall as a grand entrance to Nash's other great creation, Buckingham Palace. When the palace was extended for Queen Victoria in 1851, the great arch was moved to its present location, where as well as being an impressive entrance to Hyde Park it served as a police station until 1950.

We know that Dr Watson bought his boots in Oxford Street because he tells us so, as I observed earlier, in his introduction to the case of Lady Frances Carfax, when Holmes was 'gazing fixedly' at his boots and partly as a result of his inspection deduced that the doctor had visited the Turkish bath that day:

> 'I got them at Latimer's in Oxford Street.'
>
> 'You are in the habit of doing up your boots in a certain way. I see them on this occasion fastened with an elaborate double bow, which is not your usual method of tying them. You have, therefore, had them off. Who has tied them? A bootmaker or the boy at the bath. It is unlikely that it is the bootmaker, since your boots are nearly new. Well, what remains? The bath.'

There were many bootmakers in Oxford Street, as one might expect, but none called Latimer's. However, in the block between Orchard Street and Portman Street at number 214 was a bootmaker named John Latham. This would have been just a few minutes' walk from 221B Baker Street and the name is close to the one Watson invented, so it might be deduced that he got his boots there. At the turn of the century, when Oxford Street had been redeveloped and renumbered and was taking on something of its modern appearance (the creation of Selfridge's, for instance, was only a few years away), the name of the business changed to

Marshall and Willats, but my guess is that – even if we are right in placing the Frances Carfax case in 1902, rather than the earlier date some have suggested – Watson would still have thought of the place as Latimer's, which it had been since he had first arrived in Baker Street.

Still on the subject of boots, we find Sir Henry Baskerville shopping for them in Regent Street almost as soon as he had arrived from Canada, presumably intent on dressing himself in the manner of the English gentleman he would be expected to become. One of these new boots, in fact, would be the first to be stolen at the Northumberland Hotel.

Did Sir Henry go to one of the fashionable French bootmakers in Regent Street – there was a distinctly French flavour to the shops in general – such as Thierry or Deroy or Armand, or did he, as a countryman, buy at Holden Brothers, who specialized in 'nature true boots'? He might have stuck to what he knew and gone to the American Shoe Company or else he could have acted according to his new social status as a wealthy landowner and patronized the Regent Street branch of the prototypically English John Lobb of St James's. Even in the twenty-first century the name of John Lobb is renowned the world over for incomparable hand-made shoes, which can cost more than £2,000 a pair.

The Regent Street in which Sir Henry, and Holmes and Watson, shopped was very different from the thoroughfare we see now. One of the earliest examples of town planning in England, it was laid out and built between 1811 and 1825 to the designs of John Nash as a sort of frontier between the rather disreputable Soho and the fashionable Mayfair. Nash's stucco buildings were elegant but not particularly well constructed. For a time they suited the small shops that filled them, but by the end of the century the nature of shopping had changed, the stores needing to become larger and to offer more variety in their products for a much broader class of clientele – in short, the beginnings of the mass market. Clamour for rebuilding among retailers anxious to expand had reached a crescendo by the early 1900s, but it was not until after the First World War that work could seriously begin on the new *beaux-arts* street with its impressive façades.

Even so, Holmes and Watson would have seen the beginnings of some of the Regent Street stores which, like John Lewis of Oxford Street, would go on to become giants of retailing. Arthur Lasenby Liberty, 'china and japan merchants', was already established at number 218, next door to Mappin Brothers, cutlers and silver-smiths, which would become better known as Mappin and Webb. By Argyll Place was Dickins & Jones with nearby Swears and Wells for 'lilliputian wardrobes' (children's clothes) and, a little later, Swan and Edgar would appear.

Where Holmes's tobacconist, Bradley's, might have been, we cannot say, but we can be fairly sure that when he sent for a map of Dartmoor from what Watson heard as 'Stamford's' it was actu-ally the shop of Edward Stanford, agent for Ordnance Survey maps, in Cockspur Street, at the other side of Waterloo Place near the southern end of Regent Street. Stanfords is now in Long Acre, Covent Garden, as well as Bristol and Manchester, and advertises its main store as offering the world's largest stock of maps and travel books under one roof.

We cannot leave the West End without walking a little farther north up Regent Street, across Oxford Circus and towards Portland Place, just before which we come to Mortimer Street. It was some-where here, close to the Middlesex Hospital, that Watson was living in 1891 when Holmes appeared unannounced to prepare the doctor for a trip to the Continent to escape the wrath of the Moriarty gang.

Mortimer Street itself was almost entirely commercial at the time and in any case Watson talks of Holmes accompanying him into the garden and 'clambering over the wall which leads into Mortimer Street', so Watson's house must have been in a side-street. There are no suitable houses on corner sites, according to a contemporary map of the area, and if we are going to take seriously the phrase 'which leads into Mortimer Street', we must assume that the access was not direct. That means we are looking for an alley or a mews at the back of Watson's house.

This was a densely built-up district, full of merchants, workshops and small factories. Few of the properties enjoyed the luxury of a garden, least of all one that would offer an unseen exit. My best

Following the Trails

THESE DIRECTIONS ARE designed to allow readers – especially those who are not familiar with London – to find, if they wish, some of the more visible and visitable locations involved in the individual Sherlock Holmes cases featured in this book, either on the map or on the ground. On the basis of this, real enthusiasts who prefer to embark on longer excursions in search of Holmes sites may construct their own itineraries by grouping together the cases for which the locations are near each other or in the same area, using the indications in the relevant chapters.

The routes given here are not definitive; they are merely suggestions. The Underground is proposed for the quickest access but some bus routes are given for those who like to see more and, it must be said, to travel at a pace more reminiscent of the days when Holmes and Watson were active. Of course, to get right into the spirit of their journeys, it is probably necessary to travel by cab – or, in many cases, to walk.

'The Adventure of the Empty House'

To find Vicarage Gate, the most likely location of Dr Watson's Kensington practice, take the Underground to Kensington High Street (Circle Line). Turn right outside the station and cross Kensington High Street between Derry Street and Young Street, facing Church Street. The entrance to Vicarage Gate is a few hundred yards up Church Street on the right, just beyond the small shopping centre of Lancer Square. It was no doubt at one of the corners of these two streets where Holmes had his little bookshop. Dr Watson's apartment was probably in the short stretch of Vicarage Gate that is first on the right, though the entrance to Kensington Gardens from there is now blocked.

To follow the route to 221B Baker Street, take the Underground to Oxford Circus. Walk towards Marble Arch, turning right by the John Lewis store into Cavendish Square. From there head west up Wigmore Street then turn right into Wimpole Street and take the first left into Welbeck Way. That leads to Welbeck Street. Cross the street and take Bentinck Street then, on the far side of Mandeville Place, Hinde Street. Arriving in Manchester Square, pass Hertford House (The Wallace Collection) and turn right into Manchester Street. Follow this past George Street and turn left into Blandford Street, which leads to Baker Street. Kendall Place is on the left just before the junction. The block where 221B was situated is on the other side of Baker Street from the Blandford Street junction.

Buses to Oxford Circus 8, 10, 12, 13, 15, 23, 73, 139, 159, 453.

'The Adventure of the Six Napoleons'

To visit Pitt Street, where the journalist Horace Harker lived, take the Circle Line Underground to Kensington High Street and proceed to Church Street as above. On the left, western side of Church Street you will pass the police station from which Mr Harker summoned help on the night of the murder. Next you will pass Holland Street and then you will come to Duke's Lane. Follow Duke's Lane into Pitt Street, where the houses described by Dr Watson are on the left.

Alternatively, take the Central Line to Notting Hill Gate. Leave the station by the exit on the left of the booking hall and walk a few yards east to turn right into Church Street. Follow Church Street south to the sixth street on the right and turn into Sheffield Terrace then take the first on the left, Hornton Street.

Pitt Street is third on the left off Hornton Street. On the way you will pass the houses where, in the garden of one of them, Horace Harker's bust of Napoleon was found smashed. Follow Pitt Street across Gordon Place and you will see the 'flat-chested, respectable, and most unromantic dwellings' on your right.

Buses to Kensington High Street 9, 10.
Bus to Notting Hill Gate 390.

'The Adventure of the Bruce-Partington Plans'

Take the Underground to Gloucester Road (District or Circle Line). On leaving the station turn left then left again at the junction of Cromwell Road. Courtfield Gardens is the third street on the left, facing the line of houses in Cromwell Road that back on to the railway line. To see the backs of these houses, cross Cromwell Road and walk back towards Gloucester Road Station. At Point West, turn left and follow the narrow lane on your left past the steps to the supermarket carpark (above you on the right) and continue to the bridge that offers a view down the railway tracks towards Gloucester Road Station. Continue on your way to return to Cromwell Road, where you will walk past the houses where Hugo Oberstein lived on your way back to the station.

Buses to Gloucester Road Station 14, 74.

'The Adventure of the Blue Carbuncle'

Take the Underground (Central Line, Northern Line) to Tottenham Court Road. Walk northwards then turn right into Great Russell Street. Follow this to the British Museum, opposite which you will see the Museum Tavern ('Alpha Inn') on the corner of Museum Street. Walk down Museum Street, crossing Bloomsbury Way, to High Holborn. There, turn right towards Shaftesbury Avenue, cross the road and Endell Street will be found on the left. The old Lavery and Barraud glass factory is on the left shortly before you reach Covent Garden. Arriving in Long Acre, pass by the side of Covent Garden Underground Station and follow James Street to Covent Garden Market.

For Covent Garden Market, take the Underground (Piccadilly Line) to Covent Garden Station or Northern Line to Leicester Square.

For the Cadogan Hotel ('Hotel Cosmopolitan') take the Underground to Knightsbridge and walk south down Sloane Street. Alternatively, take the Circle or District Line to Sloane Square Station and cross the square to walk northwards up Sloane Street.

Bus to the British Museum 7.
Buses to Tottenham Court Road at St Giles's Circus (near the Underground Station) 10, 14, 24, 73, 390.
Buses to Knightsbridge 9, 10, 14, 19, 22, 52, 74, 137, 414.
Buses to Sloane Street 19, 22, 137, 452, C1.

'The Resident Patient'

For Brook Street, take the Underground to Bond Street (Central Line, Jubilee Line). Leaving the station in Oxford Street, turn right and take the first right out of the station along Davies Street. Brook Street runs right and left at the bottom of Davies Street. Brook Street can also be reached from New Bond Street.

Buses to New Bond Street 8, 10, 12, 73, 390.

'The Final Problem'

For Berners Street/Mortimer Street, take the Underground to Oxford Circus (Central Line, Victoria Line, Bakerloo Line). Follow Regent Street north to the fourth street on the right and turn into Mortimer Street. Berners Street and Berners Mews are on the right opposite the Middlesex Hospital. Alternatively, take the Underground (Northern Line) to Goodge Street. Leaving the station, turn right along Tottenham Court Road and take the first left, Goodge Street. Berners Mews and Berners Street are on the left shortly after the junction of Goodge Street and Mortimer Street.

For the site of the Lowther Arcade, take the Underground (Northern Line, Bakerloo Line) to Charing Cross. The arcade building is opposite Charing Cross Station, between Adelaide Street and William IV Street. To go on to Victoria Station, re-cross the Strand and walk down Villiers Street to Embankment Underground Station and take the District or Circle Line for three stops westward.

To visit the site of the attacks on Holmes, take the Underground to Bond Street (Central Line, Jubilee Line). Walk towards Oxford Circus and cross Oxford Street into Vere Street. At the end of Vere Street, turn left into Henrietta Street then immediately right into Welbeck Street. This will bring you to the corner of Bentinck Street, where the first attack took place.

Buses to Oxford Circus 8, 10, 12, 13, 15, 23, 73, 139, 159, 453.
Buses to Goodge Street 10, 14, 24, 73, 390.
Buses to New Bond Street 8, 10, 12, 73, 390.
Buses to Victoria Station 8, 11, 24, 38, 73.

'The Red-headed League'

Take the Underground to Barbican (Circle Line, Metropolitan Line, Hammersmith & City Line). Leaving the station, turn left and walk along Aldersgate Street to Carthusian Street and turn left again. Follow Carthusian Street into Charterhouse Street and, opposite Smithfield Market, turn right into St John Street. Follow this north for some distance, across Clerkenwell Road, to Aylesbury Street. Turn left here then take the second right into Sekforde Street, where the City and Finsbury Bank building will be found on the left towards the top of the street.

For Bridgewater Square, take the Underground to Barbican. Cross Aldersgate Street into Beech Street, almost exactly opposite, under the Bridgewater Highwalk. Bridgewater Street is on the left and leads into Bridgewater Square.

For Mitre Court, take the Underground to Chancery Lane (Central Line). Leaving the station by the Holborn south side exit, walk west to Chancery Lane and turn left. Follow Chancery Lane all the way down to Fleet Street. Here turn left and follow Fleet Street for a short distance to the corner of Fetter Lane. Mitre Court is opposite, on the south side of Fleet Street.

Bus to Barbican 43. Bus to St John Street (northern end) 38.
Buses to Fleet Street (closest stop to Fetter Lane) 15, 23.

'The Man with the Twisted Lip'

To explore the area that once contained Upper Swandam Lane, take the Underground (Northern Line, Bank branch; Jubilee Line) to London Bridge. Cross the bridge on the eastern side and go down the steps to Thames Walk, which takes you past the building that was Billingsgate Market and the Custom House, where evidence of the old wharves and cranes can still be seen. The church of St Magnus the Martyr sits on Lower Thames Street below the bridge. Alternatively, this can be reached by taking the District or Circle Line to Monument, on the north side of the river, and walking down King William Street off Fish Street Hill to Lower Thames Street. The old lanes leading to the river from Lower Thames Street have all been built over, but the sort of place that would have housed the Bar of Gold can be seen in something like its Victorian form in Lovat Lane, by the junction with Monument Street.

Buses to London Bridge 17, 21, 35, 40, 43, 47, 48, 133, 141, 149.
Buses to Monument 15, 17.

'The Disappearance of Lady Frances Carfax'

Take the Underground to Brixton (Victoria Line). Leaving the station, turn left on Brixton Road and walk south to Brixton Hill, where St Matthew's Church occupies a prominent position in the middle of the traffic system. Acre Lane, leading to Trinity Gardens, is a little further back towards the centre of Brixton, on the other side of the road from St Matthew's. Trinity Gardens is entered by taking the first turning to the right off Acre Lane.

Buses to Brixton 2, 3, 7, 35, 45, 59, 133, 159, 196, 333, 345.

The Langham Hotel, where the Hon. Philip Green was based, is in Portland Place, at the northern extremity of Regent Street and opposite Broadcasting House. Nearest Underground station Oxford Circus (Central Line, Victoria Line, Bakerloo Line).

Buses to Portland Place 88, 453, C2.

'The Problem of Thor Bridge'

Claridge's Hotel, where the Gold King J. Neil Gibson stayed, is at the corner of Brook Street and Davies Street, Mayfair. Nearest Underground station Bond Street (Central Line, Jubilee Line) – walk down Davies Street at the side of the station.

'The Adventure of the Red Circle'

Take the Underground (Piccadilly Line) to Russell Square. Leaving the station, turn left and walk up to the north-east corner of Russell Square then turn right into Woburn Place. Coram Street ('Great Orme Street') is the first street on the right, leading to Brunswick Square. At the first junction on the left you will see the house that must have been at the centre of the case, though

'A high, thin, yellow-brick edifice' in 'a narrow thoroughfare at the north-east side of the British Museum': this building in Coram Street, Bloomsbury, matches the one identified by Watson in 'Great Orme Street' in 'The Adventure of the Red Circle'

virtually everything round it has changed, including the names of the streets.

Buses to Woburn Place 59, 68, 91, 168.

'The Adventure of the Dying Detective'

Simpson's-in-the-Strand, The Grand Divan, is at 100 Strand. Nearest Underground stations are Charing Cross (Northern Line, Bakerloo Line), Embankment (District and Circle Lines) and Temple (District and Circle Lines).

Buses to Strand 6, 9, 11, 13, 15, 23, 87, 91, 139, 176.

'The Adventure of Charles Augustus Milverton'

Take the Underground (Northern Line, Edgware branch) to Hampstead. From the Underground station, walk north up Holly Hill to Frognal Rise and Branch Hill. This will bring you to Heath Road and West Heath.

Bus to Hampstead Heath 24.

'The Adventure of the Norwood Builder'

The Anerley Arms is at 2 Ridsdale Road, Anerley, Penge. A train from Charing Cross will stop at Anerley Station nearby.

'A Scandal in Bohemia'

Take the Underground to St John's Wood (Jubilee Line). St John's Wood Terrace is a little south of the station, off Wellington Road. The barracks are in Ordnance Hill, leading off St John's Wood Terrace.

Buses to St John's Wood 36, 187.

'The Adventure of the Retired Colourman'

The Theatre Royal Haymarket is, of course, in Haymarket. Nearest Underground stations Piccadilly Circus (Piccadilly Line, Bakerloo Line), Leicester Square (Piccadilly Line, Northern Line), Charing Cross (Northern Line, Bakerloo Line).

Buses to Haymarket via Shaftesbury Avenue 14, 19, 38.
Buses to Piccadilly 8, 9, 14, 19, 22, 38.
Buses to Piccadilly Circus via Regent Street 3, 6, 12, 13, 15, 23, 44, 88, 139, 159, 453.
Bus terminates Piccadilly Circus 22.

'The Adventure of the Noble Bachelor'

To visit Gordon Square take the Underground to Euston Square (Circle Line, Metropolitan Line) or to Euston Station (Northern Line, Victoria Line), which is 200 yards from Euston Square. Cross Euston Road by the Wellcome Centre and walk along Gordon Street, which leads directly to Gordon Square.

Buses to Euston 10, 18, 30, 73, 205, 390.

To visit the site of the former Métropole Hotel take the Underground to Embankment (District and Circle Lines). Exit on to Victoria Embankment and turn right, passing under the bridge to Northumberland Avenue. The Métropole building is at the river end of the avenue, the one with the semi-circular tower on the corner of Whitehall Place.

Alternatively, take the Northern or Bakerloo Lines to Charing Cross. Northumberland Avenue is on the west side of the station, off Trafalgar Square. From there walk towards the river, passing the sites of the former Grand Hotel on the right and of the former Victoria Hotel – now called the Grand – farther down on the left side of the street.

Buses terminate Trafalgar Square/Charing Cross 29, 91.

'The Adventure of the Second Stain'

To visit Lord North Street take the Underground (District and Circle Lines, Jubilee Line) to Westminster. Pass the Houses of Parliament and walk along Millbank to Great Peter Street. Turn right here and Lord North Street will be found on the left, leading to Smith Square.

Buses to Millbank/Parliament Square 3, 87.

'The Adventure of the Illustrious Client'

For Berkeley Square take the Underground to Green Park (Piccadilly Line, Victoria Line, Jubilee Line) or to Bond Street (Central Line, Jubilee Line). From Green Park cross Piccadilly to Berkeley Street and continue to Berkeley Square. From Bond Street follow Davies Street, by the side of the station.

Bus to Berkeley Square via New Bond Street or Davies Street 8.
Buses to Green Park 9, 14, 19, 22, 38.

The Café Royal is at 68 Regent Street. Nearest Underground station Piccadilly Circus (Piccadilly and Northern Lines).

Buses to Regent Street 3, 6, 12, 13, 15, 23, 44, 88, 139, 159, 453.

'The Adventure of the Three Garridebs'

For Seymour Street ('Little Ryder Street') take the Underground to Marble Arch (Central Line). Walk in a westerly direction along Oxford Street to Edgware Road. The short northern section of Seymour Street is on the western side of Edgware Road, leading to Connaught Square.

Buses terminate Marble Arch 30, 159. Other buses to Marble Arch 2,
10, 16, 36, 73, 74, 82, 137, 148, 414, 436.

'The Greek Interpreter'

For a tour of Pall Mall and club land in Holmes's footsteps, take the Underground to Green Park (Piccadilly Line, Jubilee Line, Victoria Line). Leave the station on the south side of Piccadilly and walk east towards Piccadilly Circus. Turn right into St James's Street and follow this down to Pall Mall. Along Pall Mall, turn left into St James's Square, where Watson went to study Chinese porcelain at the London Library.

To 'walk round the corner to Whitehall', go to the eastern end of Pall Mall and turn right into Waterloo Place and follow this to the steps at the Duke of York Memorial. Entrance to Whitehall via Horseguards Road, Downing Street and King Charles Street is restricted for reasons of security, so at the bottom of the Duke of York steps turn left along The Mall to Spring Gardens and Charing Cross, turning right into Whitehall.

Buses to Green Park 9, 14, 19, 22, 38.

'The Adventure of the Three Gables'

For White's Club, where Langdale Pike sat at the bow window, take the Underground to Green Park (Piccadilly Line, Jubilee Line, Victoria Line) and follow the directions as above to St James's Street.

Buses to Green Park 9, 14, 19, 22, 38.

A Study in Scarlet

The Criterion is on the south side of Piccadilly Circus (Underground).

St Bartholomew's Hospital (Bart's), where Dr Watson met Sherlock Holmes for the first time, is in West Smithfield, London EC1. Nearest Underground stations are Barbican (Circle Line, Metropolitan Line), Farringdon (Circle Line, Metropolitan Line), Blackfriars (District Line, Circle Line) and St Paul's (Central Line).

From Barbican turn right outside the station and right again into Long Lane, which runs into Smithfield. The hospital is opposite the market buildings across the square.

From Farringdon follow Cowcross Street to Smithfield Market or Farringdon Road to West Smithfield.

From Blackfriars, the most direct route to Bart's is to cross Queen Victoria Street outside the station and follow St Andrew's Hill and Creed Lane to Ludgate Hill, where St Paul's Cathedral is on the right. Turning towards the cathedral, cross Ludgate Hill and walk north on Maria Lane and Warwick Lane to Newgate Street. Turn right here and cross the road to King Edward Street, which leads to Little Britain and the back of the hospital. The main entrance is signposted from here.

From St Paul's Underground Station take the Newgate Street exit and cross to King Edward Street, following the directions above.

Buses to Bart's Hospital 4, 8, 25, 56, 172, 242.

The courtyard of St Bartholomew's Hospital. It was in the hospital laboratory that Dr Watson first met Sherlock Holmes in the winter of 1880–1

BLOOMSBURY

Take the Underground to Holborn (Central Line, Piccadilly Line) or Russell Square (Piccadilly Line). From Holborn cross to Southampton Place, the site of Dr Watson's first practice, and continue north across Bloomsbury Way into Bedford Square. The Royal Pharmaceutical Society building is at the north-west corner. Turn left here and cross the road to Montague Street, alongside the British Museum. From Russell Square take Bernard Street to Russell Square. Montague Street begins at the south-west corner of the square. Holmes's lodgings are at the further end from here.

Nearby is the restored Victorian pub the Princess Louise, at 208–9 High Holborn.

Buses to Bloomsbury Way 1, 8, 19, 25, 38, 55, 98, 242.
Buses to Russell Square 1, 188.
Bus to Great Russell Street 7.

BAKER STREET

To see the building which stands on what we have established must have been the block containing 221B, take the Underground to Marble Arch (Central Line) or Bond Street (Central Line, Jubilee Line). Baker Street is on the northern side of Oxford Street more or less equidistant from the two stations, approached via Orchard Street and Portman Square.

For the statue of Sherlock Holmes and the Sherlock Holmes Museum take the Underground to Baker Street (Circle Line, Metropolitan Line). The Holmes statue is outside the main Marylebone Road entrance of the station. The museum is in what used to be Upper Baker Street, round the corner from the station, close to the junction with Park Road.

Buses to Baker Street (Oxford Street) 2, 13, 30, 74, 82, 113, 139,
    189, 274.
Buses to Baker Street (Park Road) 13, 82, 113, 274.

Index

Page numbers in *italics* refer to illustrations
Page numbers with a star* refer to quotations